SCOTLAND

NORTH
SEA

Berwick-
upon-Tweed

1

Norham

Holy Island

Cornhill-
on-Tweed

Ford

Belford

Farne Islands

2 Bamburgh

1 Beadnell

Wooler

816
The Cheviot

Eglingham

**THE
COAST**

Cheviot Hills

NORTHUMBERLAND
NATIONAL PARK

Alnwick

4 Rothbury

THE HILLS

Amble **1**

A68

3

602
Peel
Fell

Otterburn

Elsdon

6

Kielder
Water

Falstone

5

Ashington

Morpeth

2

Bellingham

Cambo

Blyth

Wark

Belsay

Cramlington

A68

Ponteland

North Shields

South
Shields

7

**ALONG HADRIAN'S
WALL**

3

Haltwhistle

Hexham

Corbridge

A69

2

8

R.Tyne

Newcastle
upon Tyne

9

Gateshead

Sunderland

Rowland's
Gill

Washington

584
Three
Pikes

Allendale

Stanley

Chester-
le-Street

Seaham

Blanchland

Consett

**CITIES &
SAINTS**

Allenheads

A68

A691

Peterlee

St John's
Chapel

Stanhope

Durham

Crook

R.Wear

WEAR & TEES

Bishop
Auckland

Sedgefield

Middleton-in-
Teesdale

Newton
Aycliffe

A1(M)

Barnard
Castle

10

Darlington

A67

Hartlepool

Stockton-
on-Tees

Middlesbrough

Penrith

Northallerton

AA **LEISURE** GUIDE

Northumbria

Author: David Winpenny
Verifier: David Winpenny
Managing Editor: David Popey
Project Management: Bookwork Creative Associates Ltd
Designers: Liz Baldin of Bookwork and Andrew Milne
Picture Library Manager: Ian Little
Picture Research: Liz Allen, Alice Earle, Carol Walker and Lesley Grayson
Cartography provided by the Mapping Services Department of AA Publishing
Copy-editors: Marilynne Lanng of Bookwork and Pamela Stagg
Internal Repro and Image Manipulation: Sarah Montgomery
Production: Rachel Davis

Produced by AA Publishing
© AA Media Limited 2007
Reprinted 2008
Updated and revised 2010

Published by AA Publishing (a trading name of AA Media Limited, whose registered office is Fanum House, Basing View, Basingstoke, Hampshire RG21 4EA; registered number 06112600).

 This product includes mapping data licensed from the Ordnance Survey® with the permission of the Controller of Her Majesty's Stationery Office. © Crown Copyright 2011. All rights reserved. Licence number 100021153.

ISBN 978-0-7495-6691-3
ISBN 978-0-7495-6704-0 (SS)

A CIP catalogue record for this book is available from the British Library.

The contents of this book are believed correct at the time of printing. Nevertheless, the publishers cannot be held responsible for any errors or omissions or for changes in the details given in this book or for the consequences of any reliance on the information it provides. This does not affect your statutory rights. We have tried to ensure accuracy in this book, but things do change and we would be grateful if readers would advise us of any inaccuracies they may encounter.

We have taken all reasonable steps to ensure that the walks and cycle rides in this book are safe and achievable by people with a realistic level of fitness. However, all outdoor activities involve a degree of risk and the publishers accept no responsibility for any injuries caused to readers while following these walks and cycle rides. For more advice on walking and cycling in safety see pages 16–17.

Some of the walks and cycle routes may appear in other AA books.

Visit AA Publishing at theAA.com/shop

Printed and bound in China by C&C

A04393

CONTENTS

Welcome to...

Northumbria

Northumbria is a secret kingdom – a place barely discovered by tourists yet one of the most magically beautiful parts of Britain. It encompasses a vast swathe of northeast England, from the fiercely contested Scottish Border to the boundary of Yorkshire; from the High Pennines – England's last wilderness – to the golden sands along Northumberland's coast.

It includes the smooth Cheviot Hills and the rugged Simonsides, deep river valleys, expansive Kielder Water and huge tracts of forest, as well as vibrant Newcastle upon Tyne, historic Durham, the long valleys of the Tees and Wear, and the fascinating industrial history of the Tyne.

The borderlands were fiercely fought over for centuries: Stone Age and Iron Age men dug hilltop forts here to protect their lands, and at places like Yeavering Bell you can see the result. Here you will find superb examples of boulders carved with prehistoric patterns – with good specimens at Old Bewick – and the tradition was kept alive when Christianity came with Saxon crosses, as at Rothbury. Northumbria in the Dark Ages was a beacon of piety and learning; great saints – St Aidan, St Cuthbert, and St Godric among them – ministered here, and the Venerable Bede, from whose Ecclesiastical History we have many of the saints' stories, lived at Jarrow.

A few centuries before Bede, the Roman emperor, Hadrian, constructed a wall across Northumbria to control entry to his empire; Hadrian's Wall is still a startling sight, snaking its way across the countryside, a symbol of immense military power. The great medieval lords also showed their prowess by building castles as protection from Scottish raiders; the area has some of the best, such as Warkworth, Dunstanburgh, Bamburgh and Raby. The area has fostered inventors, too, including George Stephenson and Lord Armstrong. Northumbria's heroine, Grace Darling, celebrated for rescuing nine shipwrecked sailors, lived her short life on – and off – the coast, and native artistic life is represented by the renowned 19th-century wood engraver Thomas Bewick and romantic novelist Catherine Cookson.

Many visitors come as much for the scenery as for formal attractions. If you want to get away from it all, Northumbria offers you the chance, whether it's walking in the hills, or lying on an empty beach of glorious sand, this is the place to come. But keep the secret – Northumbria is where only those in the know will return, as often as they can.

SCOTLAND

Berwick-
upon-Tweed

1

Norham

Cornhill-
on-Tweed

Holy Island

Farne Islands

Ford

Belford

2 Bamburgh

1 Beadnell

Wooler

816
The Cheviot

C h e v i o t   H i l l s

Eglingham

**THE
COAST**

NORTHUMBERLAND

NATIONAL PARK

Alnwick

4

Rothbury

Amble **1**

THE HILLS

3

NORTH
SEA

602
Peel
Fell

*Kielder
Water*

Otterburn

Elsdon
6

Falstone

5

2

Bellingham

Cambo

Morpeth

Ashington

Wark

Belsay

Blyth

**ALONG HADRIAN'S
WALL**

Cramlington

Ponteland

North Shields

South
Shields

7

3

Haltwhistle

Hexham

Corbridge

2

8

R Tyne

**Newcastle
upon Tyne**

9

584
Three
Pikes

Allendale

Rowland's
Gill

Gateshead

Sunderland

Stanley

Washington

Blanchland

Consett

Chester-
le-Street

Seaham

Allenheads

**CITIES &
SAINTS**

St John's
Chapel

Stanhope

R Wear

Durham

Peterlee

WEAR & TEES

Crook

Penrith

Bishop
Auckland

Sedgefield

Middleton-in-
Teesdale

Newton
Aycliffe

Stockton-
on-Tees

Barnard
Castle

10

Darlington

Hartlepool

Middlesbrough

Galashiels

Keiso

Jedburgh

Northallerton

6 Walk start point

1 Cycle start point

2 Tour start point

ESSENTIAL SIGHTS

View Dunstanburgh Castle from Embleton Bay...walk the Elizabethan ramparts of Berwick-upon-Tweed...take a boat trip to the Farne Islands...sample a pair of oak-smoked kippers in Craster...climb up Yeavering Bell to see the ancient hill-fort and take in the wide-ranging view...drive on the road over Harthope Moor from St John's Chapel to Langdon Beck – one of England's highest roads...follow the Pennine Way from Widdy Bank Farm to Cauldron Snout waterfall...view Hadrian's Wall from Highshield Crags...cross and recross the magnificent bridges in Newcastle's centre...sit and contemplate in the nave of Durham Cathedral.

1 Dunstanburgh Castle
Dramatically sited on cliffs above the sea, the castle was built by the Earl of Lancaster in the 14th century. Later, John of Gaunt fortified it further. Dunstanburgh was severely damaged by Yorkist forces during the Wars of the Roses. It finally fell into ruin in the 16th century.

2 Harthope Moor
Northumbria's moorland has unmissable opportunities for walking and wildlife spotting.

3 Berwick-upon-Tweed
The ancient border town of Berwick has a series of ramparts built in the mid-16th century to replace medieval defences in the face of threats from Scotland and France.

4 Farne Islands
The National Trust-owned islands are a special attraction for birders – puffins are a favourite.

5 Alnwick Castle
Superbly preserved, Alnwick remains in the hands of the Percy family, owners since 1309.

6 Holy Island
Also called Lindisfarne, windswept Holy Island is accessible via a causeway from the mainland only twice each day. Check the tides before you travel.

6 Pennine Way
The Pennine Way is a 270-mile (435km) route from the Peak District in the south to the Scottish Borders in the north, by way of the Yorkshire Dales and Northumbria. Some brave walkers attempt the entire distance.

7 Beamish
At Beamish, the living museum re-creates everyday life and work in the north of England as it was in the early 19th century and the first decades of the 20th century. Each detail of life, work and education is accurately reproduced.

8 Hadrian's Wall
Hadrian ordered his Governor to construct a wall to prevent the warlike tribes further north from attacking the Border towns and his troops, and to mark the northern boundary of his empire.

9

9 Newcastle

The Tyne is crossed here by its famous bridges. The futuristic Millennium Bridge from Quayside stands in front of the Tyne Bridge, the Swing Bridge and, in the distance, Robert Stephenson's High Level Bridge of 1849.

10 Durham

Durham's majestic cathedral towers above the city close to the River Wear. St Cuthbert's grave can be found here, although the buildings date from almost 100 years after his remains were transported here from Holy Island.

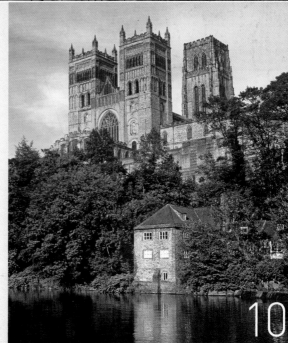

10

DAY ONE

For many people a weekend break or a long weekend is a popular way of spending their leisure time. These four pages offer a loosely planned itinerary designed to ensure that you make the most of your time, whatever the weather, and enjoy the very best the area has to offer.

Friday Night

Stay in or around Bamburgh – Waren House Hotel, 3 miles (4.8km) west is a fine Georgian house in wooded grounds overlooking Budle Bay. If you prefer village-inn type accommodation, the Blue Bell Hotel at Belford is highly recommended. Take an evening stroll around Bamburgh village and view its magnificent medieval castle (right) in the fading light and look for Grace Darling's grave in the churchyard.

Saturday Morning

In the morning you could take a walk around Bamburgh before driving along the coast road to Seahouses to take a boat trip from the busy harbour around the Farne Islands – fascinating for both children and adults. Reminders of saints from the Dark Ages abound here, but most visitors come to view the wildlife, including seals and seabirds – puffins, fulmars, petrels, kittiwakes, guillemots, oystercatchers, terns and cormorants. Don't forget to wear a hat, and perhaps your oldest clothes – the birds are notoriously good shots!

Saturday Lunch

On dry land, a late lunch calls. Among the good eating places in Seahouses, the Olde Ship Hotel is recommended. There is a lounge where children are welcome and a small garden.

Saturday Afternoon

Drive south to Beadnell and then head inland, cross the A1 near North Charlton and take the minor road over the hills to Ros Castle, which offers really stunning views of the coast and the Cheviot Hills. Continue south through Old Bewick and on to the B6346 through Eglingham into Alnwick. The castle, with its Harry Potter associations, is wonderful inside and out – or you can just enjoy the craft shops and bustle of this lively town.

From Alnwick take the B6341 southwest through Edlingham to the A697. Turn south towards Newcastle.

Saturday Night

If your budget will stretch to it, treat yourself to a night at the Linden Hall Hotel, north of Longhorsley on the A697. Set in 450 acres (182ha), it is a luxurious country house with its own first-class restaurant, lively pub-restaurant and an enormous range of sport and leisure activities. Morpeth, 6 miles (9.7km) south, offers plenty of alternatives.

BAMBURGH

HEXHAM

BLANCHLAND

DAY TWO

The second day of your weekend visit to Northumbria offers a great house, a castle and a garden, Roman antiquities on Hadrian's Wall, lunch in Hexham and a visit to the exciting city of Durham.

Sunday Morning

Drive to Morpeth centre, then take the B6524 through Edlington and Whalton (where, at dusk on 4 July, villagers follow an old tradition and light a great bonfire – the Baal Fire – on the village green) to Belsay, with its unusual 19th-century Greek-style house, 14th-century castle and pretty garden.

Then drive up the A696 towards historic Otterburn for 5 miles (8km), turn left on the B6342, cross the A68 and take the A6079 through Chollerton. Then go right to join the B6318, which runs beside (and sometimes on top of) Hadrian's Wall. Follow signs for Chesters fort – with one of the best-preserved Roman bath houses on the Wall.

If it's wet, go straight to Hexham and head for the shelter of the shops, many of which have Victorian frontages.

Sunday Lunch

Back to the A6079 and into Hexham for lunch. There is plenty of choice in and around the town, but one good place is Dipton Mill Inn, just south of the town, which offers a wide selection of food, including local cheeses. Children are welcome and there is a pleasant garden.

Sunday Afternoon

After lunch, leave Hexham on the B6306 over the hills to see the perfect village of Blanchland, a cluster of stone houses built for the lead miners in the mid-18th century and beautifully preserved by the Trustees who own the estate.

Continue beside the Derwent Reservoir to Edmundbyers, where you join the B6278 to Consett, and eventually pick up the A691 into Durham.

An official World Heritage Site, Durham has a spectacular setting high above a loop of the River Wear. At the heart of the city are the magnificent cathedral and the nearby castle, which is now used by the university, and there are delightful old streets to explore and museums and galleries to visit.

INFORMATION

Route facts

MINIMUM TIME The time stated for completing each route is the estimated minimum time that a reasonably fit family group of walkers or cyclists would take to complete the circuit. This does not allow for rest or refreshment stops.

OS MAP Each route is shown on a map. However, some detail is lost because of the restrictions imposed by scale, so for this reason, we recommend that you use the maps in conjunction with a more detailed Ordnance Survey map. The relevant map for each walk or cycle ride is listed.

START This indicates the start location and parking area. This is a six-figure grid reference prefixed by two letters showing which 62.5-mile (100km) square of the National Grid it refers to. You'll find more information on grid references on most Ordnance Survey maps.

CYCLE HIRE We list, within reason, the nearest cycle hire shop/centre.

❶ Here we highlight any potential difficulties or dangers along the cycle ride or walk. If a particular route is suitable for older, fitter children we say so here. Also, we give guidelines of a route's suitability for younger children, for example the symbol 8+ indicates that the route can probably be attempted by children aged 8 years and above.

Walks & Cycle Rides

Each walk and cycle ride has a panel giving information for the walker and cyclist, including the distance, terrain, nature of the paths, and where to park your car.

WALKING

All of the walks are suitable for families, but less experienced family groups, especially those with younger children, should try the shorter walks. Route finding is usually straightforward, but the maps are for guidance only and we recommend that you always take the relevant Ordnance Survey map with you.

Risks

Although each walk has been researched with a view to minimising any risks, no walk in the countryside can be considered to be completely free from risk. Walking in the outdoors will always require a degree of common sense and judgement to ensure that it is as safe as possible, especially for young children.
• Be particularly careful on cliff paths and in upland terrain, where the consequences of a slip can be serious.
• Remember to check tidal conditions before walking on the seashore.
• Some sections of route are by, or cross, busy roads.

Remember traffic is a danger even on minor country lanes.
• Be careful around farmyard machinery and livestock.
• Be prepared for the consequences of changes in the weather and check the forecast before you set out.
• Ensure the whole family is properly equipped, wearing suitable clothing and a good pair of boots or sturdy walking shoes. Take waterproof clothing with you and a torch if you are walking in the winter months.
• Remember the weather can change quickly at any time of the year, and in moorland and heathland areas, mist and fog can make route-finding much harder. In summer, take account of the heat and sun by wearing a hat, sunscreen and carrying enough water.
• On walks away from centres of population you should carry a mobile phone, whistle and, if possible, a survival bag. If you do have an accident requiring emergency services, make a note of your position as accurately as possible and dial 999 (112 on mobiles).

CYCLING

In devising the cycle rides in this guide, every effort has been made to use designated cycle paths, or to link them with quiet country lanes and waymarked byways and bridleways. In a few cases, some fairly busy B-roads have been used to join up with quieter routes.

Rules of the road

• Ride in single file on narrow and busy roads.
• Be alert, look and listen for traffic, especially on narrow lanes and blind bends and be extra careful when descending steep hills, as loose gravel or a poor road surface can lead to an accident.
• In wet weather make sure that you keep an appropriate distance between you and other riders.
• Make sure you indicate your intentions clearly.
• Brush up on *The Highway Code* before venturing out onto the road.

Off-road safety code of conduct

• Only ride where you know it is legal to do so. Cyclists are not allowed to cycle on public footpaths (yellow waymarks). The only 'rights of way' open to cyclists are bridleways (blue markers) and unsurfaced tracks, known as byways, which are open to all traffic and waymarked in red.
• Canal tow paths: you need a permit to cycle on some stretches of tow path (www.waterscape.com). Remember that access paths can be steep and slippery so always push your bike under low bridges and by locks.
• Always yield to walkers and horses, giving adequate warning of your approach.
• Don't expect to cycle at high speeds.
• Keep to the main trail to avoid any unnecessary erosion to the area beside the trail and to prevent skidding, especially in wet weather conditions.
• Remember to follow the Country Code.

Walk Map Legend

Preparing your bicycle

Check the wheels, tyres, brakes and cables. Lubricate hubs, pedals, gear mechanisms and cables. Make sure you have a pump, a bell, a rear rack to carry panniers and a set of lights.

Equipment

• A cycling helmet provides essential protection.
• Make sure you are visible to other road users, by wearing light-coloured or luminous clothing in daylight and sashes or reflective strips in failing light and darkness.
• Take extra clothes with you, depending on the season, and a wind/waterproof jacket.
• Carry a basic tool kit, a pump, a strong lock and a first aid kit.
• Always carry enough water for your outing.

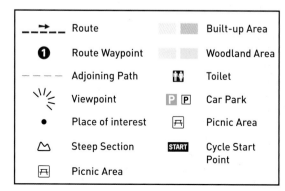

--▸-- Route		Built-up Area	
❶ Route Waypoint		Woodland Area	
— — — Adjoining Path		🚻 Toilet	
Viewpoint		P P Car Park	
• Place of interest		🏚 Picnic Area	
⌂ Steep Section		START Cycle Start Point	
🏚 Picnic Area			

BAMBURGH BEACH

The Coast

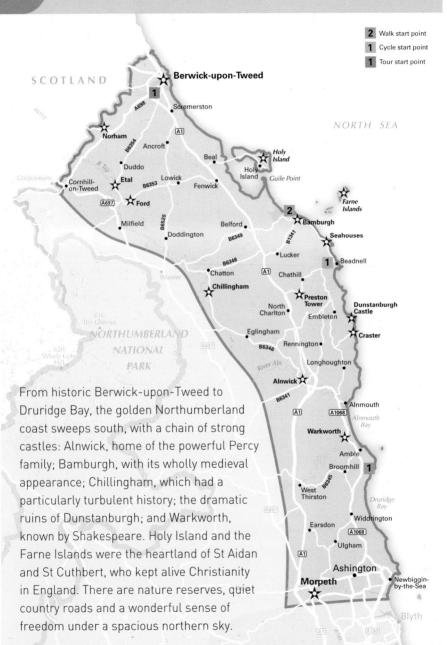

2 Walk start point
1 Cycle start point
1 Tour start point

SCOTLAND

Berwick-upon-Tweed

Scremerston

NORTH SEA

A698

A6172

A1

Norham

Ancroft

B6354

R Till

Duddo

Beal

Holy Island

Coldstream

Cornhill-on-Tweed

Etal

B6353

Lowick

Fenwick

Holy Island

Guile Point

A697

Ford

B6525

Farne Islands

Milfield

Belford

Bamburgh

Doddington

B6349

Seahouses

B1341

Lucker

Beadnell

B6348

Chatton

A1

Chathill

Wooler

Chillingham

North Charlton

Preston Tower

Dunstanburgh Castle

Embleton

NORTHUMBERLAND

Eglingham

Craster

NATIONAL

816 The Cheviot

Rennington

PARK

B6346

River Aln

Longhoughton

620 Windy Gyle Hill

Alnwick

B6341

Alnmouth

A1

A1068

Alnmouth Bay

Warkworth

Amble

Broomhill

West Thirston

B6345

Druridge Bay

A697

Widdrington

Earsdon

A1068

Ulgham

A1

Ashington

Newbiggin-by-the-Sea

Morpeth

Blyth

A1

A185

From historic Berwick-upon-Tweed to Druridge Bay, the golden Northumberland coast sweeps south, with a chain of strong castles: Alnwick, home of the powerful Percy family; Bamburgh, with its wholly medieval appearance; Chillingham, which had a particularly turbulent history; the dramatic ruins of Dunstanburgh; and Warkworth, known by Shakespeare. Holy Island and the Farne Islands were the heartland of St Aidan and St Cuthbert, who kept alive Christianity in England. There are nature reserves, quiet country roads and a wonderful sense of freedom under a spacious northern sky.

Unmissable attractions

Admire the view of Dunstanburgh Castle from Embleton Bay...take the circuit around Berwick Ramparts...take a boat trip to the Farne Islands...pay a visit to the ancient Chillingham Wild Cattle...spend a day at Alnwick Castle with its Harry Potter associations...at Lindisfarne Castle, sit in the Walled Garden...spend time watching seals from a boat or from the coast...look for mute swans on the Tweed near Berwick...ferry across the River Coquet to Warkworth Hermitage...lunch on kippers at the Craster Restaurant...go paddling at Alnmouth – or at any of the other wonderful beaches...learn about the heroic story of Grace Darling at Bamburgh.

1 Holy Island
The ruins of Lindisfarne Priory, built in 1083, stand on Holy Island. Monastic life began much earlier in AD 635 when the King of Northumbria gave this island to St Aidan. Also known as Lindisfarne, it became a leading centre of Christianity.

2 Farne Islands
Birds breeding on the Farne Islands include petrels, eiders, kittiwakes, terns, cormorants and the ever-popular puffins.

3 Alnwick Castle
This popular castle has become more widely known after appearing as Hogwarts in some of the Harry Potter films. There is a lot to appeal to children here, including Knights' Quest, where they can dress up and learn about jousting and swordfighting.

4 Alnwick Gardens
The wonderful gardens, overseen by the Duchess of Northumberland, are a major attraction in their own right. The Grand Cascade is the stunning centrepiece to the project that is still developing and improving.

5 Chillingham Castle
Chillingham Castle shows little sign of the years of neglect that were wiped away in its excellent restoration in the late 20th century. It is reputed to be England's most haunted castle.

6 Bamburgh
Best known for its castle, Bamburgh has a sandy beach that is popular in summer.

ALNWICK MAP REF NU1813

Alnwick (pronounced 'Annick') has been the stronghold of the powerful Percy family since 1309. They went on to become the Earls of Northumberland, then in the 18th century, the Dukes of Northumberland. Alnwick Castle's strong walls and round towers, although altered over the centuries, owe their outline to the Normans. Its barbican – the best surviving in Britain – and the impressive gateway, with stone figures mimicking an ever-watchful garrison, were added when the Percys arrived.

The medieval interior was completely transformed into a Renaissance palace by the 4th Duke in the 19th century. It glows with fine woodwork and marble and is filled with treasures, including paintings by Canaletto, Titian, Van Dyck and Andrea del Sarto. There are two stunning cabinets made for Louis XIV, and two great Meissen dinner services. The castle grounds are famous now as Hogwarts in the Harry Potter films.

◼ Visit

ALNWICK FOLK

If you're in Alnwick in early August, you might come across groups of brightly dressed people speaking eastern European or Scandinavian languages. They will be part of the annual Alnwick International Music Festival. It's a chance for folk musicians and dancers – mainly from the Balkans ad around the Baltic, but also from further afield and always the top performers in their countries – to demonstrate their skills. The dancing is often to the sound of unusual instruments alongside violins and accordions, such as cimbalom and bagpipes.

The park was landscaped by the renowned designer 'Capability' Brown, a Northumberland man. It is now home to the spectacular new gardens created by the Duchess, complete with a restored great cascade, hundreds of fountains and the world's biggest tree house.

Alnwick Castle cannot be said to dominate the attractive stone-built town, but its influence is apparent. The 15th-century parish church lies near the castle, while at the other end of town is a survivor of the town walls begun in 1434, the narrow Hotspur Gate, named after the most famous member of the Percy family, Shakespeare's Harry Hotspur. From the park gate you can walk to the gateway to Alnwick Abbey and continue beyond that to peaceful Hulne Priory, now a stately ruin.

Alnwick's cobbled market place bustles with life, and there are plenty of shops selling local produce, crafts and antiques. The former railway station houses one of Britain's largest second-hand book shops. Opposite the station is a column which was erected in gratitude by farmers when the 3rd Duke lowered their rents. The 4th Duke raised them again, and the column subsequently became known as Farmers' Folly.

The pastures below the castle are the scene for a mammoth Shrove Tuesday football match, which uses the Lion and Denwick bridges as goals.

BAMBURGH MAP REF NU1734

Bamburgh for most visitors means the castle, dominating both the village and the coast. It looks so completely medieval that film crews use it as a backdrop to historical romances or adventures. Yet the castle is both more and less historical than it looks. The great Whin Sill crag has been defended since the Iron Age; the crag became the site of a fort for the invading Anglians in AD 547 and was given by King Ethelfrith to his wife Bebba – Bebba's burgh became Bamburgh.

An eventful progress through the centuries ensued: Northumbrian kings were crowned here, the fortress was sacked by the Vikings, then fell easily to the Normans, who began the stone castle we now see. The great keep was built in the 1150s, and additions were made in later centuries, creating a castle that was virtually impregnable until in 1464 during the Wars of the Roses, when it became the first castle to be taken by artillery. It was Edward IV's army that shelled it into submission.

The shattered remains passed to the local Forster family during the reign of King James I of England (James VI of Scotland) and they held it – but largely left it in a derelict state – until the early 18th century, when Lord Crewe, the Bishop of Durham, took charge. He undertook some repairs and left the castle as a charitable trust, overseen by Dr John Sharpe. The good doctor then restored the ruins and ran a free school, an infirmary, a free lending library and a windmill that sold cheap flour – its tower can still be seen in the grounds.

The castle was sold in 1894 to Lord Armstrong, eminent Victorian inventor and industrialist. It is his restorations that make the castle seem so complete today. The State Rooms now appear late

Victorian, and although they are palatial, particularly the Great Hall with its impressive hammer-beam roof and musicians' gallery, they do not live up to the promise of the exterior. However, there is a fine display of arms and armour, family portraits, furniture and porcelain – as well as the chains used by Dr Sharpe's early coastguard and lifeboat service.

Bamburgh village can be extremely busy at the height of the tourist season, but it is a pleasant place for a stroll. Its parish church stands on the site of the chapel used by St Aidan and has a beautiful early 13th-century chancel and Forster family monuments, as well as the much-visited grave of the Victorian heroine Grace Darling in the churchyard. Bamburgh also has an attractive sandy beach and a spectacularly sited golf course at Budle Point, with views to Holy Island. Budle Bay, an area of wetland west of Bamburgh, is a nature reserve visited by many wildfowl – information boards will help you to identify them.

BERWICK-UPON-TWEED

MAP REF **NT9953**

Berwick-upon-Tweed was a Royal Burgh of Scotland until William the Lion surrendered it to the English in 1174. Over the next 300 years it changed hands 11 times, became a free town in 1482 and an independent state within England in 1502. It became legally part of Northumberland only in 1974.

Such a turbulent past gives Berwick its own gritty individuality. A fascinating town, it holds a unique place in both British and military history. In the Middle Ages it was protected at its north end by the castle, first mentioned in 1160 and rebuilt at the end of the 13th century. Its White Wall plunges from the castle to the river, protecting precipitous steps known locally as 'The Breakynecks'. The Constable's Tower is impressive, and you can see part of the northwest wall from the station platform – much more was demolished when the railway arrived.

Berwick had medieval town walls – the best remaining stretch lies alongside the cliffs between Meg's Mount and the railway bridge – but more important are its Elizabethan ramparts. Built between 1558 and 1569, when the Scots and the French were threatening England, they are unique in Britain. The walk along them should not be missed, to see the 22-foot high (6.7m) stone-faced walls, 12 feet (3.6m) thick at the base and topped with grassed mounds. They were never properly finished. In 1568 Mary, Queen of Scots, fled to England, thus removing some of the Scottish threat – and when Scottish king James VI became James I of England in 1603 they were redundant.

Berwick remained a military town, however, and Britain's earliest barracks, dating from the early 17th century, were built to house nearly 600 men. They now house two museums – the King's Own Scottish Borderers Museum and the town Museum and Art Gallery, which, alongside exhibits of local history, has something of a surprise – outstanding works of art, including paintings by Degas and Daubigny, medieval carvings and Chinese ceramics. Modern art is displayed at the Gymnasium Gallery, which is found on the Parade.

Opposite the Barracks is Berwick parish church – rare as it was built in the 1650s, during the Commonwealth. Oliver Cromwell, who was a friend of the benefactor, hated bells, so there is no tower. Bells did arrive in Berwick, but were hung in the mid-18th century Guildhall, Berwick's most prominent building, with its tall tower and spire.

Among Berwick's many landmarks are its bridges. Successive early wooden bridges were swept away. Without one for 200 years, Berwick put up another wooden bridge in Tudor times, but it was King James VI, going to London in 1603, who demanded, and eventually paid for, the magnificent 1,164-foot long (355m) Old Bridge. It remained the only road bridge in the town until the Royal Tweed Bridge was built in 1928, but the most spectacular of Berwick's bridges, Robert Stephenson's Royal Border Bridge, 2,152 feet (656m) long on 28 high arches, was built for the railway in 1846.

Tweedmouth's neighbour, Spittal, has a good beach, and Berwick harbour is busy with both leisure and commercial boats.

Northumberland's Coast and Hills

Castles, spectacular views of the Cheviots, wild moorland and the coastal islands are among the highlights of this circular drive from England's most northerly town. Extend the drive by 10 miles (16km) if you visit Holy Island, but check on the tides.

Route Directions

Start at the historic town of Berwick-on-Tweed.

1 From the centre go over the Royal Tweed Bridge, signed 'Newcastle, A1' and go right, signed 'Coldstream A698'. Head right at the first roundabout and then straight on at the second, following Coldstream signs. After 3 miles (4.8km), turn right along an unclassified road signed 'Horncliffe, Norham Castle'. In 2 miles (3.2km) pass the ruins of Norham Castle to enter Norham. Norham Castle was one of the strongest border castles.

2 Follow the road past the cross and at the T-junction turn left, signed 'Berwick', on the B6470. After 0.5 miles (800m) turn right along an unclassified road. At the T-junction turn left on the A698, to Berwick, then fast right on to an unclassified road, signed 'Felkington'. Follow this road for 4 winding miles (6.4km), following signs for Etal and Ford, to reach the B6354, where you turn right. Follow the road for 3 miles (4.8km) through Etal to Ford.

In Ford, visit Lady Waterford Hall, with murals depicting locals in Biblical scenes.

3 Just before Ford church go right, signed 'Kimmerston'. After 1.5 miles (2.4km) turn right at the T-junction, signed 'Milfield'. Go over Redscar Bridge and straight on to meet the A697, where you turn left towards Wooler and Morpeth. Follow the main road through Akeld and at a junction a mile beyond turn right (signed 'Wooler light traffic only'), then continue into the centre of Wooler. This bustling market town is popular with walkers.

4 At the end of the main street turn left by the church then cross the main road on to the B6348, signed 'Chatton', 'Belford' and 'Chillingham Castle, Wild Cattle'. After 2.5 miles (4km) there is a sharp right-hand bend at the top of a hill. Beyond this, follow the main road for 2.5 miles (4km) to Chatton. Turn right at the 'Chillingham, Alnwick' sign. Follow the road past the

entrance to the Wild Cattle Park and the castle.

5 At the brow of the hill turn left to 'Hepburn Wood Walks'. Follow the road through Hepburn and uphill, past Ros Castle. The gated narrow road needs care as it winds for 7 miles (11.3km) – wide verges allow passing. The road drops into North Charlton. At the A1 turn left and after a mile (1.6km), turn right, signed 'Preston Tower, Ellingham'. After 2 miles (3.2km) you will see the 1392 Preston Tower. This has a medieval Border life display.

6 At the T-junction just beyond, turn left to 'Beadnell, Seahouses'. Go over the level crossing at Chathill, continue for 3.5 miles (5.7km) past Beadnell and along the coast on the B1340, into Seahouses. At the first roundabout turn right, at the next roundabout turn left, following 'Coast' signs to ancient Bamburgh. Bamburgh has a huge, square Norman castle.

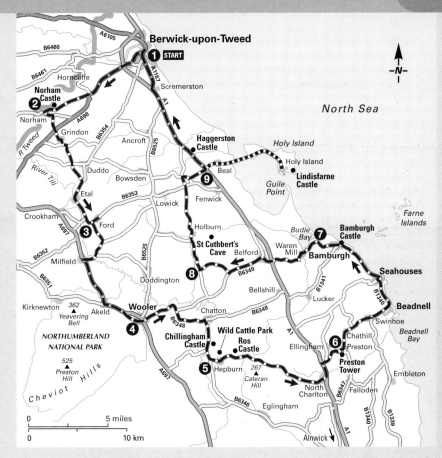

7 Go round Budle Bay and at the T-junction in Waren Mill turn left to 'Belford, Wooler'. In 2.5 miles (4km) turn right on the A1 and left to 'Belford'. Just before the church go left on the B6349 to 'Wooler'. In 2.5 miles (4km), turn right on a narrow unclassified road signed 'Hazelrigg, Lowick'. There are spectacular views of the Cheviots from here.

8 Turn right at a T-junction after 2 miles (3.2km), to 'Holburn, Berwick'. A little way along is the track to St Cuthbert's Cave. After 5 miles (8km) cross the B6353, then after 0.5 miles (800m) turn right to 'Kentstone, Beal'. At the A1 go straight over to visit Holy Island.
Lindisfarne has a ruined priory and a Tudor castle.

9 Otherwise, turn left towards Berwick, passing Haggerston Castle. In 4.5 miles (7.2km) go right at the roundabout along the A1167 to 'Scremerston, Berwick'. At the next roundabout go straight on, over the bridge and into the town centre.

CHILLINGHAM MAP REF NU0525

Chillingham village, with its Tudor-style houses, was built by the Earls of Tankerville, related by marriage to the Grey family. In the church the tomb of 15th-century Sir Ralph Grey has some rare figures of saints that escaped later religious destruction. The Greys' fortress, Chillingham Castle, was started in 1245, but much of its present appearance dates from 1344.

By then the park wall had been in existence for 124 years. Inside it was a herd of early wild cattle. Their descendants, a very rare survival, still roam within the walls. They have white coats; their muzzles and horn tips are black. Only the dominant bull sires calves; when eventually defeated by one of the younger males he is banished to a distant part of the park. The park is open to the public, though a good view of the cattle cannot be guaranteed – binoculars will help.

The castle was nearly lost after the contents were sold in 1933 and it was left empty. There was a fire when soldiers were billeted here in the 1940s and rot ravaged the rest, until Sir Humphrey Wakefield, related to the Greys, bought the castle in the 1980s and began its triumphant restoration.

Visitors can see the splendid Great Hall, with banners and armour, as well as antique furniture, tapestries and restored plaster- and metalwork. There is even a torture chamber, suitable for a place reputed to be 'the most haunted castle in England'. The gardens include woodland walks and a topiary garden on the site of the tournament ground.

CRASTER MAP REF NU2519

A picturesque village that seems almost to tumble into the sea, Craster became a haven for fishing in the 17th century, although its harbour, today used by pleasure craft and traditional cobles, was given its present form in the 1900s. It was built by the local landowners – the Crasters – in memory of Captain Craster, killed on an expedition to Tibet in 1904. The harbour exported whinstone (used for roads and kerbs), and you can still see the concrete arch that once supported the chipping silos. The quarry is now the National Trust car park, a good starting point for walks to Dunstanburgh Castle.

Howick Gardens, a mile (1.6km) south of Craster, surround a late 18th-century house (not open), which was the home of the 2nd Earl Grey. As Prime Minister, he steered through the 1832 Parliamentary Reform Bill – and gave his name to Earl Grey tea; sample it in the Earl Grey Tea House. There is fine woodland with a network of paths and glades where rare plants and shrubs thrive – don't miss the rhododendron season – as well as lawns, a terrace with urns, and alpine beds.

DUNSTANBURGH CASTLE
MAP REF NU2622

The ruins of Dunstanburgh Castle are among the most romantically sited in Britain. Back in medieval times the sea surrounded the steep cliffs to the north of the castle and swelled into the moat which had been dug around its more vulnerable sides. In area it is the largest castle in Northumbria, 11 acres (4.4ha) and was begun in 1314 by Thomas, Earl

of Lancaster to protect a small harbour. His great gatehouse, largest of all the surviving fragments, was turned into a keep by John of Gaunt in the 1380s. He built a new entrance to the west, making the castle less easy to attack. Taken and recaptured several times in its history, it finally fell into ruin in the 16th century. Dunstanburgh is said to be haunted by Sir Guy the Seeker, who failed to waken an enchanted princess here.

ETAL & FORD

MAP REFS **NT9339/NT9437**

Etal and its neighbour Ford have all the ingredients for a good family day out. Etal boasts Northumberland's only thatched pub, the Black Bull, and the Post Office serves teas with real home baking. The village's main street is a pretty mix of thatched and stone-tiled cottages, and leads to Etal Castle, the ruins of a border tower-house of the early 14th century. Scottish guns were

dragged back to damaged Etal after the Battle of Flodden, and an exhibition in a former chapel located in the grounds has displays about that battle and the Border Wars in general.

In nearby Heatherslaw the water-powered corn mill is an 18th- and 19th-century building on a site used for more than 700 years. Here, milling is demonstrated, and stone-ground flour and locally baked products are on sale. Heatherslaw also boasts a 15-inch (38cm) gauge steam railway that runs for almost 2 miles (3.2km) alongside the River Till from the mill to the castle.

Ford owes much of its model village atmosphere to Louisa, Countess of Waterford, who lived at Ford Castle and spent most of her widowhood caring for the villagers. The 14th-century castle (not open) was added to during the 18th century – the Portcullis Gate dates from 1791 – and in the 1860s by the Countess of Waterford. She was a famous beauty (she met her husband at the Eglinton Tournament in Ayrshire in 1839) and a friend of artists. Lady Waterford Hall, commissioned as the village school, has murals of Biblical scenes she painted in watercolour on paper, using locals as her models – the joiner's son as Jesus and her gamekeeper as St Paul. She was also responsible for the blacksmith's forge, with its horseshoe doorway. A memorial to the Countess can be found in the churchyard quite near to the church entrance.

Etal and Ford and their surrounding villages have a wide variety of craft, food and plant shops, and opportunities for fishing and riding.

◼ Visit

THE BATTLE

The Scots gathered for battle on Flodden Hill, 4 miles (6.4km) west of Ford, but the Earl of Surrey sent part of his force to cut off the Scots' retreat northwards. James IV might have won if he had launched his attack during this manoeuvre, but he delayed fatally and faced the attack from the north, near Branxton. Fighting began at 4pm and by nightfall the Scots had been defeated, despite brave fighting. Among the dead were James and his son, twelve earls, 15 clan chiefs, a bishop and two abbots – as well as 5,000 English. The site of the battle is marked with a modern cross, inscribed 'FLODDEN 1513. TO THE BRAVE OF BOTH NATIONS'.

HOLY ISLAND MAP REF NU1241

Holy Island has been known by this name since the 11th century, although its Celtic name, Lindisfarne, is just as familiar. This was one of the main centres of Christianity in the Dark Ages. The island was given to St Aidan in AD 635 by the King of Northumbria, and it became respected throughout Europe.

Even more famous and influential was St Cuthbert, whose life and teaching were a magnet for pilgrims. He died in AD 687 and was buried in the church. When it was sacked during Danish raids in AD 875 the monks fled with his bones, searching for a safe and permanent home for them. The remains arrived in Durham more than 100 years later.

Lindisfarne seems an ideal setting for the monastic life – bare, windswept and flat, surrounded by sands covered by the sea twice daily. Before crossing to the island via the causeway, check the tides – here, in the Tourist Information Offices, in the local newspapers, or on the internet – and note any warnings. A refuge is provided for the foolhardy who don't. The old pilgrims' route from the mainland is marked by posts leading almost directly to the village.

South of the square is St Mary's Church. Nearby in the Heritage Centre there is an electronic copy of the famous Lindisfarne Gospels (with 'turnable' pages)– the original is in the British Museum. It was illuminated here in AD 698. Just offshore is St Cuthbert's Island, used by the saint when he needed total solitude. It can be reached at low tide, and a simple cross marks the site of his chapel.

Next to the church are the remains of Lindisfarne Priory, built of beautiful red sandstone, weathered into gullies and ripples. It was founded by the Bishop of Durham in 1083, and finished by 1140. Its columns, like Durham Cathedral, are patterned with zig-zags and chequers. The remaining rib of the crossing, known as the rainbow arch, shows that it once had a strong tower. Part of the cloister remains – in contrasting grey stone – but there is not much more, except a gatehouse and defensive walls against the Scots. The nearby museum tells the story of the island.

Stones from the Priory were used in the 1540s to build a fort on Beblowe, a rocky crag on the south shore. The fort's purpose was to defend the harbour, where part of Henry VIII's fleet had taken shelter in 1543 and where today the boats of the lobster and crab fishermen mingle with the pleasure craft. These defences were never tested before peace with the Scots came 60 years later. Apart from its capture for one night in 1715 by two opportunist Jacobites, it was neglected until Edward Hudson, founder of *Country Life* magazine, bought it in 1902 and commissioned architect Edwin Lutyens to adapt it for use as a home.

Now owned by the National Trust, it shows Lutyens at his most inventive, hollowing rooms out of unexpected corners, some like the inside of an upturned stone boat. The Upper Battery gives fine views of the island, the Farne Islands and the mainland. Lutyens' gardening collaborator Gertrude Jekyll designed the tiny walled garden 500 yards (457m) north of the castle.

Around Druridge Bay

This walk takes in a nature reserve, country park and beach. The biggest attraction here is the variety and numbers of birds that visit these coastal lakes. Resident populations are joined by those migrating between the summer feeding and breeding grounds in the far north and Africa, where many over-winter. Wimbrel, dunlin and sanderling are among the migrating species, while redshank, plover and bar-tailed godwit spend the winter here. You will also see whooper and Bewick swans as well as many favourites such as tits, finches, blackbirds and robins.

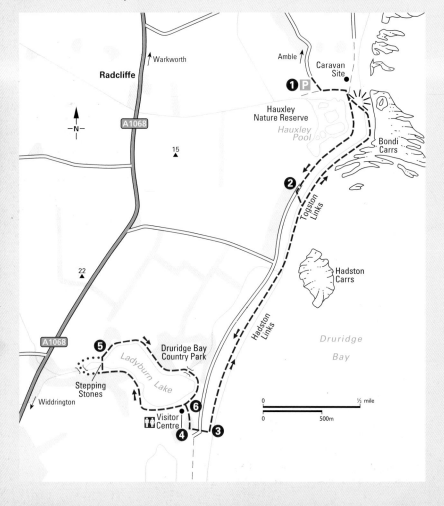

Route Directions

1 A waymarked footpath beside the car park entrance winds between the nature reserve and a caravan site towards the coast. Through a gate at the bottom, turn right on a track, which shortly passes two gates that give access to bird hides overlooking the lake.

2 Leaving the reserve, continue a little further along a tarmac track to an informal parking area on the left, where there is easy access on to the beach. Now, follow the shore past Togston Links, across a stream and on below Hadston Links.

3 After 1.25 miles (2km), wooden steps take the path off the sands on to the dunes. Cross a tarmac track and continue over a marshy area into pinewood. Beyond the trees, emerge by a car park and walk across to the Druridge Bay Country Park visitor centre, where there is a café and toilets.

4 A footway to the left winds around Ladyburn Lake, soon passing a boat launching area. Keep to the lower path, which soon leads to stepping-stones across the upper neck of the lake. If you would rather not cross here, continue around the upper edge of a wooded nature sanctuary above the water to a footbridge higher up. Over the bridge, turn immediately right, through a gate into a nature sanctuary. Follow the river bank back though another gate to reach the far side of the stepping-stones.

5 This side of the lake has a more ´natural´ feel, the path winding through trees to emerge beside a lushly vegetated shoreline where swans like to feed. After crossing a bridge over the lake's outflow, carry on back to the visitor centre.

6 Retrace your steps to the beach and turn back towards Hauxley, but when you reach the point at which you originally dropped on to the sands, remain on the shore towards Bondi Carrs. Seaweed can make the rocks slippery, so be careful clambering over them as you round the point, where Coquet Island then comes into view ahead. Not far beyond there, after passing a look-out post and approaching large rocks placed as a storm defence, leave across the dunes, retracing your outward path the short distance back to the car park and the start.

Route facts

DISTANCE/TIME 5.5 miles (8.8km) 1h45

MAP OS Explorers 325 Morpeth & Blyth; 332 Alnwick & Amble

START Car park at Hauxley Nature Reserve, grid ref: NU282024 (on Explorer 332)

TRACKS Paths and tracks, with good walk on beach, no stiles

GETTING TO THE START Turn off the A1068 just south of Amble into the village of High Hauxley. Follow the road through the village as it takes a sharp turn to the right, and then continue straight ahead to Low Hauxley. At the end of the road is the Hauxley Nature Reserve car park.

THE PUB Widdrington Inn, Morpeth. Tel: 01670 760260 (beside a roundabout on the A1068, about 4 miles/6.4km to the south)

❶ Check tides; complete coastal section not always passable at high water

Bamburgh Coast and Castle

On this walk you can enjoy a fine beach, rolling countryside and superb views to Bamburgh Castle and the Farne Islands. For as long as people have navigated this coast, the Farne Islands have been a hazard, claiming countless lives. They form two main groups of around 30 tilted, low-lying islands, some barely breaking the waves. The first attempt to mark the islands for shipping was around 1673, when a signal fire was lit on a 16th-century tower on Inner Farne. Sadly, the lights were unable to prevent every disaster. The event that caught the imagination of the country, though, was the wreck of the SS *Forfarshire* in 1838 because of the unstilted heroism of the Longstone keeper William Darling and his daughter Grace in rescuing the survivors.

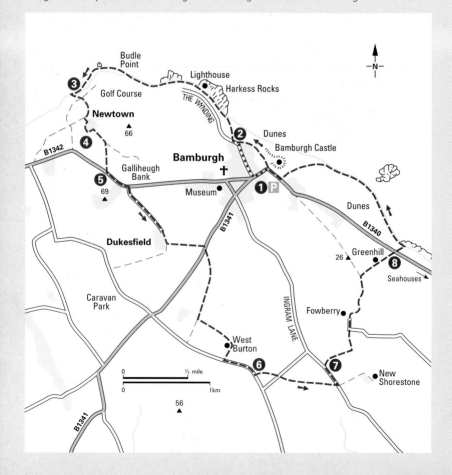

Route Directions

1 Walk towards Bamburgh village, where you'll find the museum and church. Our route, however, continues along the beach, reached either across the green below the castle or by following The Wynding, just beyond, then crossing the dunes behind.

2 To the left, the sand soon gives way to Harkess Rocks. Carefully pick your way round to the lighthouse at Blackrocks Point, which is more easily negotiated to the landward side. Continue below the dunes, shortly regaining a sandy beach to pass around Budle Point.

3 Shortly before a derelict pier, climb the dunes towards a Second World War gun emplacement, behind which a waymarked path rises on to a golf course. Continue past markers to a gate, leaving along a track above a caravan park. At a bend, go through a gate on the left (with a blue 'Coast Path' marker) and continue along the field edge to reach the cottages at Newtown.

4 Beyond, follow a field boundary on the left to regain the golf course through a kissing gate at the top field corner. Bear right to pass left

of a look-out and continue ahead on a grass track to the main road.

5 Turn left and walk down Galliheugh Bank to a bend and turn off to Dukesfield. Approaching the lane's end, go left over a stile and walk past a house, crossing two stiles in the field's far corner. Then continue by a hedge to a road. Cross to follow a green lane opposite and eventually, just after a cottage, reach a stile on the left. Make for West Burton farm, turn right through the farmyard to a lane, then go left.

6 Beyond a bend and over a stile on the left, signed 'New Shorestone', bear half right across a field. Emerging on to a quiet lane, go over another stile opposite and continue in the same direction to reach Ingram Lane.

7 Some 300yds (274m) to the left, a gated track on the right leads away, then around to the left towards Fowberry. Meeting a narrow lane, go left to the farm, then turn right immediately before the entrance on to a green track. In the next field, follow the left perimeter around the corner to a metal gate. Through that, remain beside the right-hand

wall to a double gate, there turning right across a final field to Greenhill. Keep ahead to the main road.

8 Continue across to the beach and head north to Bamburgh. Approaching the castle, turn inland, over the dunes, where a cattle fence can be crossed by one of several gates or stiles. Work your way through to regain the road by the car park.

Route facts

DISTANCE/TIME 8.5 miles (13.7km) 3h15

MAP OS Explorer 340 Holy Island & Bamburgh

START Pay-and-display parking by Bamburgh Castle, grid ref: NU183348

TRACKS Field paths, dunes and beach, 11 stiles

GETTING TO THE START Bamburgh lies on the B1342 between Belford and Seahouses. Bamburgh Castle is just outside the town, on the coastal side of the road, where you will find a pay-and-display car park.

THE PUB Lord Crewe Arms Hotel, Front Street, Bamburgh.
Tel: 01668 214273

MORPETH MAP REF NZ1986

Morpeth's town centre has attractive alleys and courtyards, and some fine old buildings, including the Town Hall by Vanbrugh, rebuilt after a fire in the 19th century, and the Clock Tower found in the middle of Oldgate, erected in the early 17th century. Before the days of bypasses, the 19th-century bridge used to carry the A1 traffic over the River Wansbeck into the town. In the bridge chapel, the Chantry, with its tea room and Tourist Information Centre, more than 60 craftsmen display their work. Don't miss the fascinating Bagpipe Museum, also on the premises.

St Mary's Church is where you will find the best example of stained glass in the whole of Northumberland, dating, like the church, from the 14th century. Its churchyard, with a watchhouse to prevent body snatching, contains the grave of Suffragette Emily Davison, who died when she threw herself under the hooves of George V's horse at the 1913 Derby meeting. St James's Church, three quarters of mile (1.2km) north, is a superb Victorian neo-Norman building.

Morpeth has had two castles. The earlier, on Ha' Hill near St Mary's, was not rebuilt after King John burned the town in 1261. Of the second, on Castle Walk, parts of the wall and a gatehouse, mostly 15th-century, survive. Near by in Carlisle Park is the Courthouse, once the gateway to the gaol.

Mitford, west of Morpeth, has a fine church in woodland and the remains of a mainly 12th-century castle. Nearer to Morpeth is Newminster Abbey, one of the richest Cistercian abbeys in the north, with vast sheep runs on the Cheviots. Little remains today except part of the Chapter House, set among grass, wild flowers and brambles.

NORHAM MAP REF NT9047

Renowned 19th-century artist J M W Turner often painted the attractive ruins of Norham Castle, which guards an important ford across the Tweed into Scotland. Built about 1158, Norham was the Bishop of Durham's chief northern stronghold – the area was known as Norhamshire and was part of County Durham, not Northumberland. The great red sandstone keep was battered into surrender by the Scottish army before Flodden, and the Marmion Gate is a reminder that Sir Walter Scott set his poem about the battle here. In 1209 the Scottish king, William the Lion, agreed to pay tribute money to King John here and the castle was besieged unsuccessfully for 40 days by Alexander II five years later. Edward I declared himself Paramount King of Scotland at Norham, where Robert the Bruce and John Baliol were chosen finalists in the King of Scotland competition.

In the village, St Cuthbert's Church shows the rich influence of the Durham Bishops, with a chancel of about 1170 and Norman nave arches like part of Durham Castle. The 17th-century vicar's stall and pulpit were once in Durham Cathedral. The cross set on the village green has a medieval base and 19th-century top. Norham Station (open by appointment) has a working signal box, a good model railway and a fine collection of Victoriana.

PRESTON TOWER

MAP REF **NU1827**

Robert Harbottle's pele tower, which was built in the 1390s, suffered the ignominy of having two of its four towers demolished in 1603, 90 years after Sir Guiscard Harbottle died at Flodden in hand-to-hand fighting with the Scottish king, James IV. It was rescued from decay and encroaching farm buildings in 1864, but only so that it could hold water tanks for the Georgian house near by.

The tower has a more dignified existence today, housing displays about the Battle of Flodden and its impact, as well as re-creating the uncomfortable and spartan life of the Border Reivers at the beginning of the 15th century.

SEAHOUSES & THE FARNE ISLANDS MAP REFS **NU2231/NU2338**

In 1858 Seahouses was referred to as 'a common-looking town, squalid in places', but today it has a much more prosperous air, geared to the tourist industry. In the town there are some pleasant fishermen's cottages around Craster Square and a busy harbour that was originally built in the 18th century, but was much enlarged in the 19th. Seahouses harbour is the place to get boat trips to the Farne Islands, and there are fine sands to the north and the south of the sheltering Snook Point.

A mile (1.6km) south of Seahouses is Beadnell, which has an 18th-century church and a pub – the Craster Arms – with a large carved coat of arms on its front wall and the remains of a medieval tower at the back. Above the harbour – the only one on the east coast that faces

west – is the site of the medieval St Ebba's chapel and a group of lime-kilns which date from 1798.

St Aidan spent each Lent on Inner Farne, one of the 28 Farne Islands (or 15, if you count at high tide), and St Cuthbert lived here from AD 676 to AD 685. His cell on Inner Farne was surrounded by an embankment so that all he could see was heaven above. The present St Cuthbert's Church on Inner Farne, near the site of his hermitage, dates mostly from about 1370 and has 17th-century woodwork which was brought here from Durham Cathedral in the 19th century.

To the west is Prior Castell's Tower, which may have held a lighthouse from the days when there were Benedictine monks on the island. Today's white-painted lighthouse, which is open to visitors, was built in 1809. Further out, beyond Staple, is Longstone, a rather uninviting, low, bare rock with a red-and-white striped lighthouse, built in 1826. This was where the Darling family lived, and from where Grace and her father set out on their rescue mission.

For many visitors the attraction of the Farne Islands is their wildlife, especially the birds and the seals. Egg collectors caused unprecedented damage in the 19th century, and the Farne Islands Association, set up in 1880, employed watchers to protect the breeding birds. The National Trust has owned the islands since 1925, and permits to land on Inner Farne and Staple Island must be bought from the Wardens. Check, too, that your boatman is licensed to land his passengers. During the breeding season, from May to July, landing is restricted – and if the weather is bad you may not be able to land at all. There are nature walks on both these islands.

The great dolerite rocks that form the Farne Islands are the easternmost part of the Great Whin Sill, and the rocks are home to at least 17 species of bird, which perch precariously on the cliffs or wheel noisily overhead – always wear a hat when visiting these islands!

The delightful little puffins are always favourites with visitors, but you may also see fulmars, petrels, razorbills, ring plover, rock pipits, eiders (known locally as St Cuthbert's – or Cuddy's – Chicks), kittiwakes, terns, guillemots, shags, cormorants, oystercatchers and, of course, gulls. The boat trips usually pass near enough to see their nesting sites, and on Staple and Inner Farne you can walk, with care, among their nests.

WARKWORTH MAP REF NU2406

Shakespeare, who set three scenes of his Henry IV here, called the ruins of Warkworth Castle 'this worm-eaten hold of ragged stone'. Actually, the huge keep is one of the most spectacular in Britain. Set in a loop of the River Coquet on the site of the original motte, its plan is a cross superimposed on a square, and it stands to its full height, partly restored in the 19th century for use by the Duke of Northumberland. The original 11th-century structure was replaced by a stone castle before 1158 and was sacked by the Scots in 1174. The Great Gate Tower, guarding the south approach, was built around 1200, as was the Carrickfergus Tower to the west. The

GRACE DARLING

Grace Darling's father was keeper of the Longstone lighthouse. Before dawn on 7 September 1838 the consumptive Grace rowed with her father out to the 400-ton luxury passenger-steamer *Forfarshire*, which had gone aground on Big Harcar in a northerly gale. Before the Seahouses lifeboat, with Grace's brother aboard, had arrived, they had saved nine lives, and young Grace became a national heroine, her fame assured by her early death four years later at the age of 27. Wordsworth wrote that she was 'Pious and pure, modest and yet so brave'. The boat used for the daring rescue, a locally built coble, 21 feet (6.4m) long, is now displayed in the Grace Darling Museum in Bamburgh.

Percys lived at Warkworth rather than Alnwick until the 16th century and the Lion Tower carries their crest.

The Percy Lion is also carved on the keep wall that dominates the little town, where the medieval street plan is still evident. Georgian and Victorian houses lead down the hill to the church and the fortified bridge. The Old Pretender was proclaimed here in 1715, his army dined at the Masons' Arms and in the church his Catholic chaplain said prayers.

The church has a 14th-century spire but inside it is almost all Norman, with a nave more than 90 feet (27.5m) long and an unusual stone-vaulted chancel, its roof ribs highly decorated with sharp-cut zig-zags. This now-peaceful church was the scene of a massacre in 1174, when the Scottish army slaughtered most of the population of Warkworth, seeking refuge within its walls.

Northumberland Coast and the Farne Islands

This is a very pleasant ride with few hills and spectacular scenery. A little offshore from this stretch of the Northumbrian coast are the Farne Islands, with thousands of grey seals. Some islands are bird sanctuaries and can be visited by boat. Inner Farne, the largest of these small islands, is home to hordes of nesting seabirds.

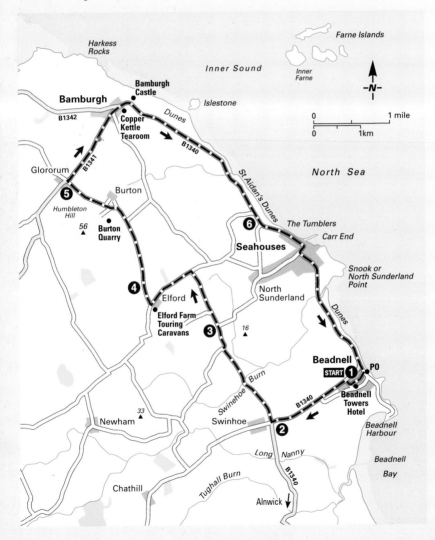

Route Directions

1 From the church in the middle of the village, pass the Village Pantry and the Craster Arms and then follow the road round to the right to reach a T-junction. Turn left on to the B1340, which is signposted to Embleton.

2 At a crossroads, just before Swinhoe, turn right on to a minor road heading towards North Sunderland. This is a pretty country lane, almost level, with hedges on each side and meadows beyond. At a junction turn right on to 'Cycle Route 1' to Seahouses and Bamburgh.

3 At the point where the road to Bamburgh turns right at a junction beside some Nissen huts, keep on cycling straight ahead along an unsigned lane. At the next T-junction turn left and pass through the little hamlet of Elford. Opposite Elford Farm Touring Caravans, turn right and head towards Bamburgh.

4 Head up a hill and at the top you will get your first brief glimpse of stunning Bamburgh Castle ahead of you on the right. At the next junction, near Burton, keep to the left and follow this lane until you reach a crossroads at Glororum.

5 Turn right back on to 'Cycle Route 1', the B1341, and keep straight ahead for Bamburgh. The castle, perched on its basalt outcrop, dominates the skyline. Cycle on through Bamburgh to a T-junction. Turn right into Church Street, go downhill past the castle entrance and continue along the coast road to Seahouses.

6 Keep left and follow the signs for Beadnell. Keep right at a roundabout then go left at the next roundabout. Continue along the coast and take the first turn left into Beadnell. Cross the main road at the Post Office and continue past a bus shelter to return to the church at the start of the ride.

Route facts

DISTANCE/TIME 13 miles (21km) 2h30

MAP OS Explorer 340 Holy Island and Bamburgh

START Beadnell, on-street parking, grid ref: NU230292

TRACKS Roads and country lanes

GETTING TO THE START
Beadnell village lies on the coast on the B1340, easily reached from the A1 between Alnwick and Berwick-upon-Tweed.

CYCLE HIRE Alnwick Cycles, 24 Narrowgate, Alnwick. Tel: 01665 606738; www.alnwickcycles.co.uk

THE PUB The Lobster Pot, Beadnell Towers Hotel, The Wynding, Beadnell. Tel: 01665 721211

■ TOURIST INFORMATION CENTRES

Alnwick
The Shambles.
Tel: 01665 510665; www.
welcomenorthumberland.
co.uk/contact

Berwick-upon-Tweed
106 Marygate.
Tel: 01289 330733; www.
welcomenorthumberland.
co.uk/contact

■ PLACES OF INTEREST

Alnwick Castle
Tel: 01665 510777;
www.alnwickcastle.com

The Alnwick Garden
Denwick Lane, Alnwick.
Tel: 01665 511350;
www.alnwickgarden.com

Bamburgh Castle
Tel: 01668 214515;
www.bamburghcastle.com

Berwick Barracks
The Parade,
Berwick-upon-Tweed.
Tel: 01289 304493;
www.english-heritage.org.uk

Berwick Castle
Berwick-upon-Tweed. Free.

Chillingham Castle
Tel: 01668 215359;
www.chillingham-castle.com

**Coquet Island,
RSPB Reserve**
Tel: 01665 711975.

Dunstanburgh Castle
Craster. Tel: 01665 576231;
www.english-heritage.org.uk

Etal Castle
Etal. Tel: 01890 820332;
www.english-heritage.org.uk

**Farne Islands &
Longstone Lighthouse**
Inner Farne and Staple
Island. Tel: 01665 721099;
www.nationaltrust.org.uk

Flodden Battlefield Trail
Branxton. Free.
www.flodden.net

Grace Darling Museum
Radcliffe Road, Bamburgh.
Tel: 01668 214910;
www.rnli.org.uk

Heatherslaw Corn Mill
Ford. Tel: 01890 820488;
www.ford-and-etal.co.uk

Heatherslaw Light Railway
Tel: 01890 820244;
www.ford-and-etal.co.uk

Lady Waterford Hall
Ford. Tel: 01890 820503;
www.ford-and-etal.co.uk

Lindisfarne Centre
Marygate, Holy Island.
Tel: 01289 389004;
www.lindisfarne-centre.com

Lindisfarne Priory
Holy Island. Tel: 01289
389200; www.english-
heritage.org.uk

Norham Castle
Tel: 01289 304493; www.
english-heritage.org.uk. Free

Paxton House
Paxton. Tel: 01289 386291;
www.paxtonhouse.co.uk

St Cuthbert's Cave
Belford. 3 miles (4.8 km)
west. Free.

**Warkworth Castle
& Hermitage**
Tel: 01665 711423; www.
english-heritage.org.uk

■ FOR CHILDREN

Chain Bridge Honey Farm
Horncliffe. Free.
Tel: 01289 386362;
www.chainbridgehoney.co.uk

Conundrum Farm
Loughend Farm, Berwick.
Tel: 01289 30800 or 306092;

Fenton Centre
Tel: 01668 216216;
www.fentoncentre.com

**Marine Life Centre and
Fishing Museum**
Main Street, Seahouses.
Tel: 01665 721257

**Sanctuary Wildlife Care
Centre**
Crowden Hill Farm, Ulgham.
Tel: 01670 791778;
www.wildlife-sanctuary.co.uk

■ SHOPPING

Alnwick
Open-air market, Thu and
Sat. Farmers' Market last Fri
of every month.

Amble
Quayside market, Sun.

Berwick-upon-Tweed
Open-air market, Wed, Sat.

Etal and Ford
Crafts, foods and plant shops.

Morpeth
Open-air market, Wed.
Farmers' market 1st Sat of
each month.

LOCAL SPECIALITIES

Crafts

Belford Craft Gallery
2 Market Place, Belford.
Tel: 01668 213888;
www.belfordcraftgallery.com

Northumbria Craft Centre
The Chantry, Morpeth.
Tel: 01670 500717;
www.morpeth.co.uk/chantry.
bpmus

FISHING TACKLE

Game Fair
12 Marygate, Berwick.
Tel: 01289 305119;
www.gamefair-flyfishing.net

Hardy and Greys Ltd.
Willowburn, Alnwick.
Tel: 01665 602771;
www.hardyfishing.com

FOOD & DRINK

L Robson & Sons Ltd
Craster.
Tel: 01665 576223;
www.kipper.co.uk
Kippers and smoked fish.

Lindisfarne Limited
St Aidans Winery, Holy Island.
Tel: 01289 389230;
www.lindisfarne-mead.co.uk
Mead, honey and fudge.

■ PERFORMING ARTS

Alnwick

Playhouse. Tel: 01665 510785;
www.alnwickplayhouse.co.uk

Berwick-upon-Tweed

The Maltings Theatre and
Arts Centre, Eastern Lane.
Tel: 01289 330999;
www.maltingsberwick.co.uk

■ SPORTS & ACTIVITIES

ANGLING

Coarse and Fly
Ask at Tourist Information
Centres and tackle shops.

Sea
Alnmouth and Amble:
enquire at harbour.
Berwick-upon-Tweed: Shore
fishing is restricted because
of seals. For boat fishing,
enquire at Berwick harbour.

COUNTRY PARKS, FORESTS & NATURE RESERVES

Amble Dunes Nature
Reserve.
Chillingham Woods and
Hepburn Wood.
Cresswell Pond Nature
Reserve, Amble.
Druridge Bay Country Park,
Amble.
Hauxley Nature Reserve.
Hulne Park, Alnwick.
Lindisfarne and Budle Bay
Nature Reserve.
Scotch Gill Wood Nature
Reserve, Morpeth.

CYCLE HIRE

Alnwick
Alnwick Cycles,
24 Narrowgate.
Tel: 01665 606738

Berwick-upon-Tweed
Cyclelife, 10 Oak Drive,
Lionheart Enterprise Park.
Tel: 01665 602925

HORSE-RIDING

Alnwick
Tel: 01665 579305;
www.shipleyequestrian.co.uk

Seahouses
Tel: 01665 720320;
www.slatehallridingcentre.com

CYCLE ROUTES AND LONG-DISTANCE FOOTPATHS

Coast and Castles Cycle Route
A 200-mile (320km) ride,
Newcastle to Edinburgh.
www.coast-and-castles.co.uk

The Northumbrian Coastline
A 61-mile (98.2km) walk from
Creswell to Berwick.

St Cuthbert's Way
A 62-mile (100km) pilgrimage
path, Melrose to Lindisfarne.
www.stcuthbertsway.fsnet.
co.uk

St Oswald's Way
A 97-mile (156km) route from
Holy Island to Heavenfield.
www.stoswaldsway.com

■ ANNUAL EVENTS & CUSTOMS

Alnwick

Shrove Tuesday Football.
Fair, late Jun–early Jul.
International Music Festival,
late Jul–early Aug.
Northumbrian Gathering,
Nov.

Berwick-upon-Tweed

Border Marches, May.
Riding the Bounds, early May.
May Fair, last Fri in May.
Curfew Run (Running the
Walls), Jul.

Morpeth

Northumbrian Gathering,
weekend after Easter.

Tea Rooms

Pilgrims Coffee Shop

Front Street, Holy Island,
Berwick-upon-Tweed
TD15 2SJ
Tel: 01289 389209;
www.pilgrimscoffee.com
Well-situated in the heart
of the village, Pilgrims is
more Continental coffee shop
than English tea room, but
offers great sandwiches
made with its own freshly
baked bread. Try the local
crab sandwiches, and some
fantastic cakes, too. You can
eat in the pretty walled
garden when the sun shines.

Copper Kettle Tea Rooms

21 Front Street,
Bamburgh NE69 7BW
Tel: 01668 214315; www.
copperkettletearooms.com
On the main street that leads
from the church to the castle,
the Copper Kettle Tea Rooms
is a delightful, cosy building,
with panelled walls, arched
windows and a pretty garden.
As well as its famous cream
teas, the café offers light
meals and snacks, including
excellent home-made soup.

Grannies

18 Narrowgate,
Alnwick NE66 1JG
Tel: 01665602394
You'll find yourself tempted
into Grannies by the
home-made cakes in the
ground floor shop – and you
can enjoy them, and more, in
the quirky tea room down the
narrow stairs. It's like an
old-fashioned kitchen
complete with granny's
bloomers drying overhead.
Locals love the scones and
teacakes – or you could
sample the delicious
Chocolate Juliette.

Pubs

The Black Bull

Etal TD12 4TL
Tel: 01890 820200
This, the only thatched pub
in Northumberland, is set on
the wide road that leads to
the ruined Etal Castle. Its
garden is a great place to
linger in the summer. As well
as a good choice of real ales,
the 300-year-old pub has
a wide and varied menu of
good, home-cooked pub food,
plus sandwiches and snacks.

Blue Bell Hotel

Market Place,
Belford NE70 7NE
Tel: 01668 213543;
www.bluebellhotel.com
The Blue Bell was once a
coaching inn, and its elegant
Georgian façade retains the
atmosphere of the age. Inside
it is smart, too, and you can
relax in the bar or bistro
where a range of up-market
bar food is available, or dine
more formally in the Garden
Restaurant. Whichever you
choose, the food is usually
top quality, and made from
fresh local ingredients.

Olde Ship Inn

Seahouses
NE68 7RD
Tel: 01665 720200;
www.seahouses.co.uk/
theoldeship/home.htm
Near the harbour, and with
such a name, the Olde Ship
inevitably has a nautical
theme. The well-kept cellar
produces a good pint, and
the inn has a hearty, mostly
traditional menu that is
strong on puddings – plum
crumble and stewed rhubarb
and custard – to revive
memories of childhood.

The Tankerville Arms

Eglingham
NE66 2TX
Tel: 01665 578444;
www.tankervillearms.com
In the heart of a quiet village
– pronounced 'Egglin–jum' –
the Tankerville Arms has
some good real ales and an
excellent menu, which
changes every month. You
can eat in one of several cosy
areas, surrounded by old
prints, listening to the talk
of local farmers.

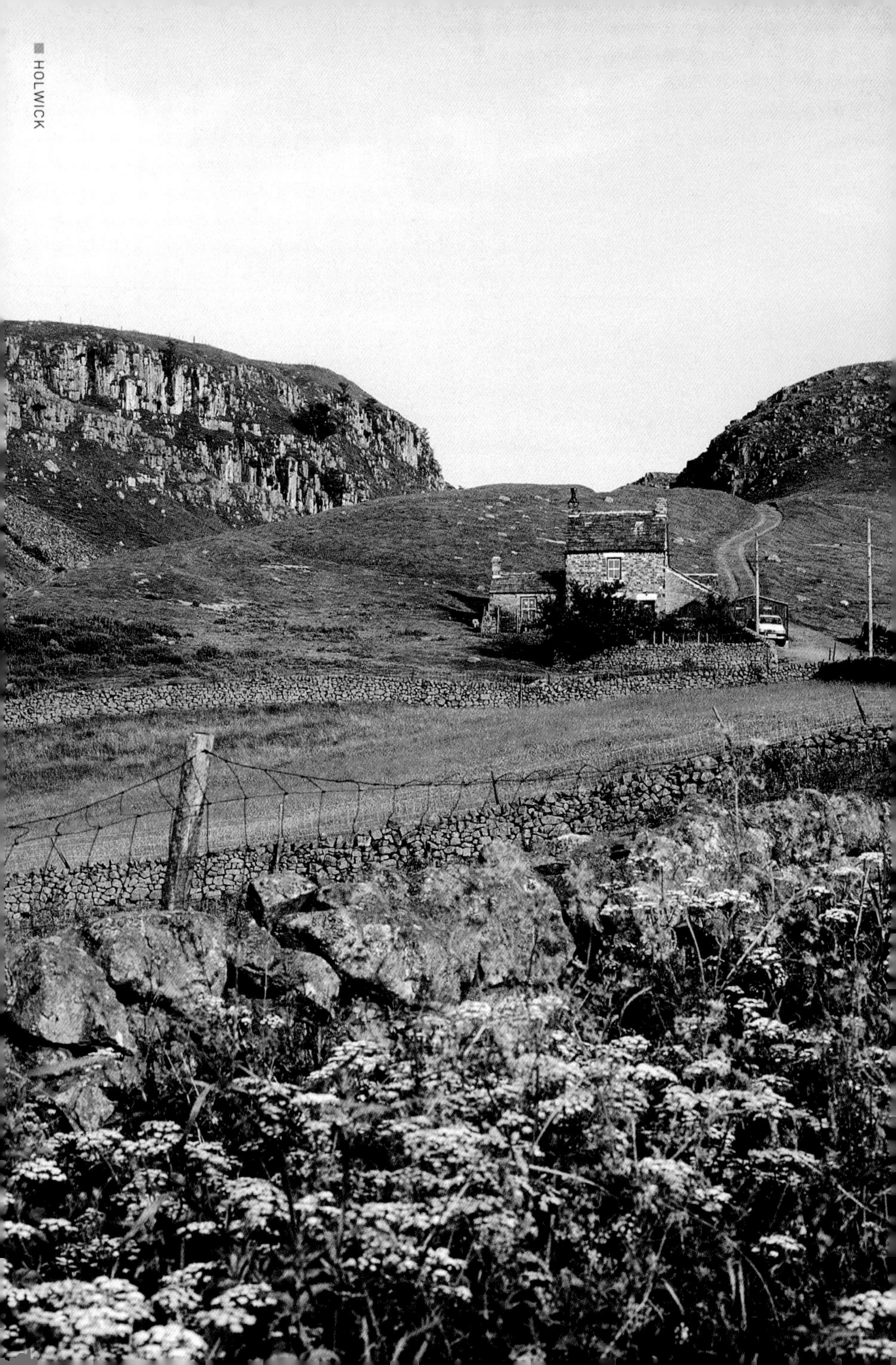

The Hills

Turbulent history and a sense of remoteness have tended to set the hills of Northumberland apart. These high, windswept moors and deep valleys were once bitterly fought over by English and Scots. Protection came from fortified bastle houses and pele towers. Now there is peace, and much of the area is protected as part of the stunning National Park.

3 Walk start point

2 Cycle start point

ROTHBURY

ELSDON

YEAVERING BELL

Unmissable attractions

Walk through the woods to Hareshaw Linn waterfall, near Bellingham...attend a concert in atmospheric Brinkburn Priory...hire a bike at spectacular Kielder Water... visit Cragside near Rothbury and see the hydroelectric scheme...try to spot a curlew on the moors near Alwinton...enjoy the colourful wall-paintings in the central hall at Wallington...climb Yeavering Bell for the views and the hill-fort...walk through the Breamish Valley...climb Simonside...imagine what it was like to be a reiver at Black Middens Bastle...pay a visit to a skilful maker of traditional Northumbrian pipes in Longframlington...spend the day at the Border Shepherds' Show, Alwinton...watch the Baal Fire celebration at Whalton...take a stroll in Happy Valley.

1 Wallington

The mansion is renowned for its Pre-Raphaelite-style murals, showing a series of events from Northumberland's history. They were executed by William Bell Scott. The design of the garden was influenced by the style of 'Capability' Brown who was born near by at Kirkharle and went to school in Cambo. Wallington is now owned by the National Trust.

2 Simonside Hills

In the Northumberland National Park, the Simonside Hills are characterised by stark crags, bogs and conifer forests. Bronze Age burials indicate this area's importance and there are signs of earlier occupation.

3 Cragside

Lord Armstrong, the Victorian inventor, built Cragside as his home and used his skills as a landscape architect to plan the extensive grounds. Cragside was the first house is the country to have electricity in every room.

4 Otterburn

An area in the Northumberland National Park, Otterburn is the site of occasional military operations, but still has enough space for exploring, walking and boating.

5 Brinkburn Priory

The large church of this Augustinian priory was built in around 1130. It lost its roof but was given a new one in the rebuilding of the 19th century. Since then it has remained largely empty but is known for its elegant proportions and wonderful stained-glass windows.

ALWINTON MAP REF NT9106

The small village of Alwinton lies in the Upper Coquet Valley and is set between the green Cheviots and the more rugged Harbottle Hills, making it a good base for exploring. Sir Walter Scott stayed at the popular Rose and Thistle while researching his heroic tale, *Rob Roy*.

Alwinton church is away from the village, on the hillside south of the river, and from its large churchyard there are wonderful views. Each October the village hosts the last of the season's traditional country shows – the Border Shepherds' Show – with sheep, fell racing and sheepdog trials.

Nearby Harbottle, another pleasant village, has a memorial fountain and the remains of a castle. The 30-foot (9m) Drake Stone, on the hillside, is reputedly a black-magic site, while Holystone Burn Wood, a nature reserve, has birch, juniper and oak woodland.

At Chew Green, 8 miles (12.9km) west of Alwinton, is one of Britain's best Roman earthworks. The remains of a fort and camp are clearly visible among the hills and you can reach the site from Redesdale when the army firing ranges are not in use – a drive with superb views along the Roman Dere Street.

BELLINGHAM MAP REF NY8383

The body of St Cuthbert, on its 100-year wanderings from Lindisfarne to Durham, was an early visitor to Bellingham (pronounced 'Bellin-jum'), the capital of North Tyne. The water in Cuddy's Well, named after him, was said to have miraculous properties and is used for baptisms in St Cuthbert's Church, a fascinating early 13th-century building. It was rebuilt in the early 17th century, when it was given its stone-vaulted roof, probably to protect it from the frequent Scots' raids. Cannon balls were found in the roof when it was restored.

Outside Bellingham's Town Hall is more evidence of fierce warfare – a gun captured at the Boxer Rebellion in China in 1900 – and the presence of army training areas is felt here today. For ten years from 1838 the town was a thriving iron and coal centre, but the industry was killed by competition from foundries nearer Newcastle upon Tyne and on Teesside. Evidence of that activity still remains in the cottages built for the workers along the banks of Hareshaw Burn, and the grassed spoil heaps on the path up to Hareshaw Linn waterfall at the head of its fine wooded gorge.

Bellingham, which hosts a famous agricultural show in August, is an excellent base for exploring the Northumberland National Park and the Kielder area. About 7 miles (11.3km) northwest of Bellingham, remote in the Tarset Burn valley, is Black Middens Bastle, one of very few which are open to the public. About 200 of these bastles (defensive stone houses) were built by wealthy farmers in the 16th century to protect their families and livestock, and Black Middens Bastle is a typical example. Bastles were usually about 35 feet (10.7m) by 25 feet (7.6m) in area, with two storeys. Animals occupied the windowless ground floor and people reached the upper floor by a removable ladder – the stone stairway at Black Middens was a later addition.

RIVER COQUET

The Ancient Spirit of the Simonsides

This walk visits a hill that had religious significance to early settlers and is now a rock climbers' playground. Many sites show evidence of human activity dating back 5,000 years. Conifer forests now cover the lower reaches of the hills, but the summit crags remain clear. As a sport, rock climbing began in Northumberland in the late 19th century and the crags of Simonside were among the first to be developed.

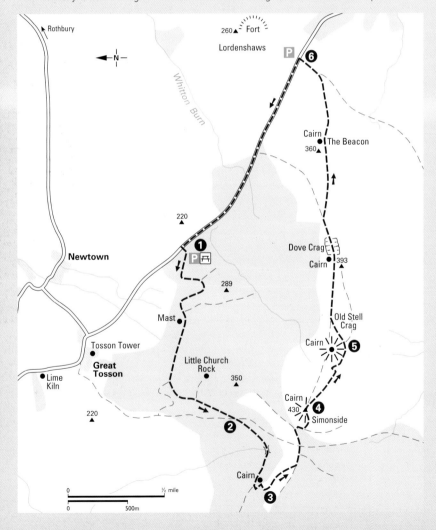

Route Directions

1 From the notice board in the picnic area, go through the gate on to the broad forest road. Follow this gently uphill, swinging to the right round the long hairpin bend, then back left at the top of the hill. When the road splits, take the right-hand fork, past the communications mast and go gently downhill. When you get to the next junction, take the left-hand fork and follow the road past the sign indicating a detour to Little Church Rock.

2 When you come to a marker post, where a narrow track leads to the left, ignore this and continue along the broad track, which now becomes grassy. After passing a huge, heavily overgrown boulder, continue to the small cairn which marks the start of a subsidiary track on the left. Follow this track uphill through the forest and out on to the heather-covered hillside. You will now see Simonside's crags 0.5 mile (800m) away to your left.

3 Continue up the narrow track to join the broader one at the edge of the upper forest and follow this left for about 275yds (251m) to the corner of the trees. A rough track, sometimes quite muddy in places, picks its way through

boulders up the hillside. Follow this, keeping the crags on your left-hand side, on to the plateau and walk on the paved route along the top of the crags to the large cairn on the summit, which is probably a burial mound.

4 Away from the summit, the track splits into two. Follow the right fork, still paved across boggy ground for a third of a mile (530m). Climb the short rise keeping the wonderfully wind-sculpted Old Stell Crag to your left and move round on to the summit and another large cairn.

5 Take the narrow path down to join the lower track. This joins the paved route again in 0.5 mile (800m), by the cairn on Dove Crag. Now descend a rocky staircase and cross a ladder stile, keeping your direction along the broad ridge path uphill to The Beacon cairn. Continue downhill for 0.5 mile (800m) to join the road at Lordenshaws car park.

6 Turn left and follow the road for 1 mile (1.6km) until you arrive back at the forest picnic area at the start the walk.

Route facts

DISTANCE/TIME
5.5 miles (8.8km) 3h

MAP OS Explorer OL42 Kielder Water & Forest

START Large car park at forest picnic area, grid ref: NZ037997

TRACKS Generally good, but steep and muddy in places

GETTING TO THE START From the centre of Rothbury, take the road out of the town through Whitton and follow it for 1 mile (1.6km) to reach Newtown. Just after the village turn left towards Great Tosson. Take the next left and follow this road into the forest. Just after entering the forest you will find the car park and picnic area on the right.

THE PUB The Queen's Head Hotel, Townfoot, Rothbury. Tel: 01669 620470; www.queensheadrothbury.com

Through the Gorge of the River Coquet

This is a fairly demanding but spectacular walk through some of Northumberland's geological history. Nowhere is this geology better laid out to view than it is around the gorge of the River Coquet, west of the village of Alwinton. To the north are the volcanic Cheviot Hills, while to the south are the fell sandstones. And in the gorge itself, at Barrow Scar, the layers of the cementstones lie fully exposed.

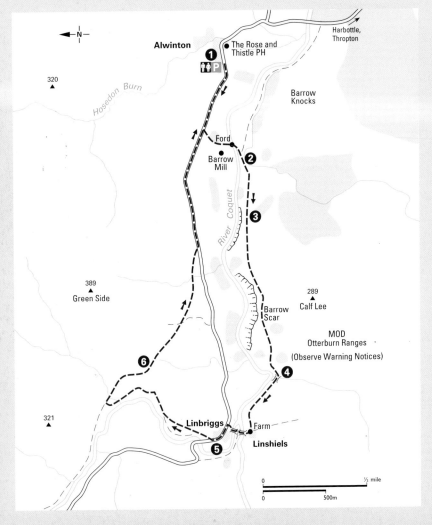

Route Directions

1 Turn right, out of the car park and follow the road for 700yds (640m) to a gate on the left leading to Barrow Mill. Go through the gate and down to the farm, passing the remains of a corn-drying kiln. Go through another gate into a field, cross this and go through a gate to the river bank. Ford the river. After rain, this will involve getting your feet wet. If the water is too high, go back to Alwinton and walk along the main road to the bridge over the Coquet. A few yards beyond, look for a stile on the right and follow the path across meadows to the ruin at Barrow.

2 Enter the field and follow the fence to the right to a gate. Go through this or over the stile about 20yds (18m) away to the left and continue to the derelict farm buildings. Follow the track up the hillside to the right-hand corner of the conifer forest.

3 About 50yds (46m) before reaching a signpost marking the edge of a military firing range, follow a less well-defined track across the heather-covered hillside to the right, rising slightly, until you come to a wire fence. Follow this over the top of Barrow Scar, keeping the

fence on your right. When you meet a second fence, follow this to a stile. Cross the stile and go down to an obvious loop in the river. In late summer, the bracken here may be deep and the track obscured.

4 At the river bend, cross a stile, then another after a further 100yds (91m). Cross over the field and a stile into the farmyard at Linshiels. Go through the farmyard, across two bridges and join the road. Turn left and follow the road until just past the farm buildings, to a signpost pointing to Shillmoor.

5 Go up the hillside, over a stile and follow the track overlooking the gorge and its waterfalls. This is the most spectacular part of the walk. For a short distance, the slopes below are quite precipitous and care is needed, though the track is good. Continue alongside the river, descending eventually to sheep pens and a ford. Continue ahead, now ascending a larger path to intersect a bridleway. Turn right and double back, crossing a stream and passing through gates before ascending the hillside on a broad sweeping path.

Route facts

DISTANCE/TIME
4.5 miles (7.2km) 3h

MAP OS Explorer OL16
The Cheviot Hills

START Car park at Alwinton, grid ref: NT 919063

TRACKS Mostly hill footpaths, some narrow, with steep drops, 8 stiles

GETTING TO THE START

Alwinton lies between the Alwin and Coquet rivers, on the edge of Northumberland National Park. From Rothbury, take the B6341 through Thropton. After 4 miles (6.4km), fork right at Flotterton, heading towards Sharperton. Cross the river, turn right and continue for 3 miles (4.8km), passing through Harbottle, until you cross the river again. Fork left, over another bridge, entering Alwinton.

THE PUB The Rose and Thistle, Alwinton.
Tel: 01669 650226

❶ Close to MOD artillery range over Barrow Scar. When red flags flying, walk may be inadvisable. Contact Range Control Officer.
Tel: 01830 520569;
www.otterburnranges.co.uk

6 At the top of the slope continue across level ground, then descend to a stile. Cross this and follow the track, over another stile and down to the road. Follow the road for a mile (1.6km) back to Alwinton.

Tarset Burn and North Tyne

The area around Lanehead is called Tarset and although the car parking area is beside Tarset Village Hall, there is in fact no Tarset village – only the burn in its valley, a parish name and the scant remains of Tarset Castle. The walks leads to the hamlet of Thorneyburn, which consists mainly of the church and the large former Rectory. The farmhouse at nearby Redhaugh probably started life as a fortified bastle house; at the edge of the field opposite is a pretty 18th-century pyramid-roofed dovecote. Sidwood Picnic Area is the start of a number of waymarked trails.

Route Directions

1 Walk to the staggered crossroads in the middle of Lanehead and turn right,

signed 'Donkleywood'. At the Redmire cottages turn right through a gate, and

cross the yard to leave by two more gates. Cross the field, passing through a gap to

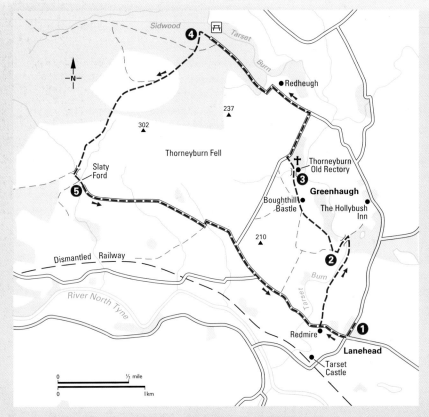

reach a handgate. Bear left, descending to a kissing gate by the river. Follow the river bank right, through a series of gates before rising to a final gate and dropping to a bridge. Cross the Tarset Burn and follow the path down a ramp to join a farm track. Turn left along this to a farmyard.

2 Go though the farmyard and ascend the track on the far side. As it bears left, go ahead past a waymarker and downhill to cross the stream. Pass another waymarked post and go through a gateway. Bend right after it and go through a hand gate. Turn left along the fence, then, at a stile, bear half right across the open moor towards the woods and church. Keep left of the ruined wall, aiming for a dilapidated shed and a wall descending to a bridge over the burn.

3 Cross the stream. Veer left on the opposite bank to locate a gate at the side of a garden. Go through this and follow the track beside the churchyard to the road. Turn right and at the T-junction turn left. Follow the lane past Redheugh farm and the 'Forestry Commission Sidwood' sign to Sidwood Picnic Area, near white-painted buildings.

4 Follow the path into the wood on the left, but after a short distance look for a right turn, crossing the burn and continuing up the hill. Cross a forest track and continue up the hill through an area of clear fell. Maintain your direction as the route levels out, now with a ditch on your right. As you begin to descend, the forest gives way to moorland on your left and you reach a gate. Continue down through the enclosure, crossing a burn then rising to a crossing track. Turn left and follow this down to cross the burn with care at Slaty Ford.

5 Continue on this prominent enclosed track to a gate. Beyond this follow the minor road for a mile (1.6km) along the flank of the North Tyne valley passing through a gate after 0.5 mile (800m) to a junction. Keep ahead, over the cattle grid and down to the bridge over the Tarset Burn. Continue on this quiet lane as it ascends the bank back to the main road. Turn left to return to your car.

Route facts

DISTANCE/TIME
7.5 miles (12.1km) 3h

MAP OS Explorer OL42 Kielder Water & Forest

START Tarset Village Hall car park, grid ref: NY 793858

TRACKS Burnside and moorland paths and tracks. Some wet areas.

GETTING TO THE START
Tarset Village Hall is in Lanehead, which is situated in the Northumberland National Park, 3 miles (4.8km) northwest of Bellingham. The road from Bellingham follows the River North Tyne and passes through Charlton before getting to the crossroads in the centre of Lanehead village, where you take a right turn to reach the village hall.

THE PUB The Hollybush Inn, Greenhaugh, Hexham. Tel: 01434 240391

BRINKBURN PRIORY

MAP REF **NU1298**

The beautiful Brinkburn Priory is set picturesquely in beech woods within a narrow valley beside the River Coquet. Augustinian canons lived here from about 1130 until Henry VIII's Dissolution. The roof of the great church fell during the 17th century, but the estate owner restored it in the mid-19th century.

A cross-shaped building with a low central tower, it has perfect proportions and round-headed Norman windows, which just become pointed Gothic here and there. The interior is mostly empty, in true medieval style. Very little remains of the rest of the monastic buildings.

ELSDON MAP REF **NY9393**

Elsdon by the River Rede was the capital of the remote Middle March – one of three protective areas set up in 1249 along the Scottish border. The large and attractive triangular green, surrounded by mainly 18th- and 19th-century houses, was once used to pen up the stock to keep it safe during border attacks. From the early 12th century the village was guarded by Elsdon Castle, built on the Mote Hills to the north by the De Umfravilles. It lasted only until 1160, when they moved to Harbottle Castle. The motte-and-bailey earthworks are the best preserved in Northumbria.

The 14th-century Elsdon Tower, once a defensive pele for the vicars of Elsdon, stands near the church. Rebuilt in the 16th and 18th centuries, it gives a strong impression of the dangers of Scots' raids. The church, another St Cuthbert's, said to be one of the places where his

body rested during its wanderings, is isolated on the green. Its bell-turret dates from 1720, but most of the building is from the 14th century. Its inside is odd, with very narrow aisles and thick walls. More than 1,000 skulls, and other bones, were found here in the 19th century – bodies of soldiers who fell at the Battle of Otterburn in 1388.

KIELDER WATER MAP REF **NY6293**

Kielder Water, at 9 miles (14.5km) long, is the largest man-made lake in Europe. Size and majesty go together here, too, with the huge Kielder Forest – the largest wooded area in Britain – coming down to the shore. At the east end is the dam, finished in 1982, which is three-quarters of a mile (1.2km) long. Complete with valve tower, it gives an idea of the scale of the undertaking.

Facilities for visitors are generous, too. Tower Knowe Visitor Centre on the southern shore is a mine of information, and you can sail the water on the ferry from here. There is also an exhibition about the area's history, as well as shops, eating places and picnic sites – as there are at Leaplish Waterside Park and at Kielder Castle Visitor Centre at the northwest end. The castle was the 18th-century shooting box of the Dukes of Northumberland.

You can drive the 12 miles (19.3km) from Kielder to Byrness along the Forest Drive – there is a toll to pay, but it is well worth it. And around both the water and the forest there are good opportunities for fishing, sailing, windsurfing, riding, mountain-biking, orienteering and simply walking along well-signed tracks.

Both Sides of the Tyne

This cycle ride takes you along both banks of the River North Tyne which has its source on Deadwater Fell in the nearby Cheviot Hills. It then flows into Europe's largest artificial lake at Kielder Water before emerging at Falstone then flowing south to join the River South Tyne at the 'meeting of waters' near Hexham. From here it continues as the River Tyne into the city of Newcastle.

This is a very peaceful route through some splendid scenery. At Kielder Water there is a range of family-friendly activities including watersports and walking trails and at this point there is the opportunity to extend this route to include some of the many cycle trails through Kielder Forest. It is also worth spending some time exploring Falstone village. The Victorian schoolroom is part of the Tynedale Renewable Energy Trail and has been converted into an excellent tea room, while the village churchyard has several interesting gravestones from the early 18th century. Look out for one depicting a girl holding hands with a skeleton. Part of the run out from Falstone takes you along the disused line of the old Borders County Railway that once ran from Riccarton Junction to Hexham. It now forms part of the Reivers Cycle Route before disappearing under water at Kielder Dam.

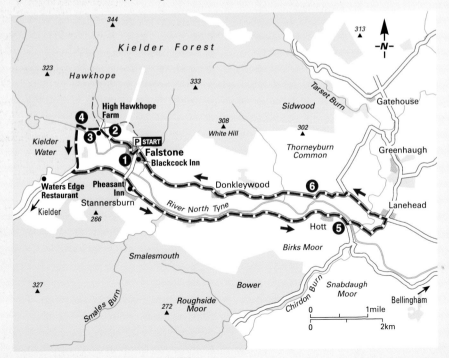

Route Directions

1 Exit the car park at the start and turn right on to a lane. Continue along it to cross a bridge by a church. The lane turns right and away from the river then forks at Mouseyhaugh. Keep left here, crossing a cattle grid, then go through a gate.

2 Cross another bridge and go through another gate then continue along the track to High Hawkhope Farm. Go through a gate and circle the right of the farmstead to reach a crossroads. Turn left on to Regional Cycle Route 10, The Reivers Route.

3 Head uphill on this broad track passing through a forestry plantation. Just before the top of the hill the trees stop and you can see along Kielder Water. On the left is a memorial erected to commemorate the opening of the reservoir by Her Majesty the Queen on 26 May 1982.

4 Continue cycling to the top of the hill and then turn left to head down to and along the road across the dam. At a T-junction with the road turn left and keep on this route, passing the Pheasant Inn to reach the Tyne Bridge after 4.5 miles (7.2km).

5 Cross the bridge and head uphill to the hamlet of Lanehead. At a junction turn left on to a narrow lane signposted to Donkleywood. This is The Reivers Route, which meanders along the edge of the Tyne valley going through several gates.

6 At one point you will cross over the old railway line at what was a level crossing, still with well-preserved gates. Beyond Donkleywood, climb to the highest point of the route before descending into Falstone. Go under a railway bridge then turn right opposite the Blackcock Inn to return to where you started.

Route facts

DISTANCE/TIME 13 miles (20.9km) 2.5 hours

MAP OS Explorer OL42 Kielder Water & Forest

START Falstone car park, grid ref: NY723874

TRACKS Minor roads, lanes and tracks

CYCLE HIRE Kielder Castle Visitor Centre, Kielder. Tel: 01434 250392

GETTING TO THE START
Take the B6320 towards Bellingham then turn left on to a minor road signposted for Kielder. Just before Kielder Water turn right following the signs to Falstone.

THE PUB The Pheasant Inn, Stannersburn, Falstone (at Stannersburn, beside the minor road from Kielder Water to Bellingham). Tel: 01434 240382

❶ Moderate hills, one short off-road section. Suitable for inexperienced riders as well as children.

NORTHUMBERLAND NATIONAL PARK

Some of the remotest and most lovely parts of Northumberland form the 398 square miles (1,030sq km) of the Northumberland National Park, which also takes in some of the best stretches of Hadrian's Wall. The area, which encompasses a long, fairly narrow area from the Cheviot Hills and the Scottish border to the most spectacular and historically interesting parts of Hadrian's Wall, has had National Park status since 1956. The Park now attracts more than a million visitors each year, but has a resident population of only around 2,500. It includes no major towns – Wooler, Rothbury, Bellingham and Haltwhistle, all natural entry points to the Park, are outside its boundaries. Only Ingram, Alwinton, Kirknewton and Elsdon offer more than a cluster of houses.

As a National Park this part of Northumberland has been recognised by the country because of its special value to the whole nation. This is wild land, of remote moorland, deep valleys and green hilltops. It's a place where one can get away from the material world and recharge the batteries, whether it's with a brisk walk, a mountain-bike ride or a time of quiet contemplation by a tumbling burn. Only along Hadrian's Wall will you find anything like a tourist hot spot – but as long as you try to avoid Housesteads fort on a sunny Bank Holiday, you're unlikely to feel crowded.

National Park status doesn't change the ownership of the land – 60 per cent of Northumberland National Park is owned privately, mostly by farmers who struggle to make a living in the difficult uplands. The Right to Roam legislation means that much of the moorland is now open for access – indeed, much of it has been open for many years, thanks to agreements negotiated with landowners by the National Park Authority. However, landowners still have the right to close land occasionally, so look out for the signs, and only wander on access land.

The National Park Authority runs visitor centres, organises walks and publishes guides and leaflets. It also supports the local farmers and offers grants for conservation purposes, such as mending stone walls and managing traditional woodland, helping them to deal with the pressures that even the most careful visitors inevitably cause.

Another 20 per cent of the Park consists of the Forestry Commission's extensive conifer plantations, many of which are open for walkers – some also have designated biking trails. Ownership of the remaining 20 per cent, however, is more controversial. The Ministry of Defence was here long before the National Park was designated in 1956, and the Army and Air Force continue to use large areas for training.

Many people consider the training areas, where live firing occurs and where tanks or camouflaged soldiers may materialise at any moment, are inconsistent with National Park status. Some argue, though, that the presence of the Forces has helped to preserve the wildness of the area; certainly there is some wildlife that thrives on the moors that might otherwise have been driven out by modern farming methods.

From Wooler, a pleasant, work-a-day place, full of local farmers and visiting walkers and fishermen, there is easy access to the great Cheviot massif lying immediately to the west and south of the town. Evidence of early settlements can be discerned all over the area, and the historic Battle Stone beside the A697 to the north of the town is a reminder of the fighting between the Scots and the English at Humbleton Hill.

To the south of the town are two beautifully wooded valleys, Happy Valley and Harthope Valley, which was formed by Harthope Burn flowing through a fault in the hills. You can drive through Earle and the delightfully named Skirl Naked as far as Langleeford, where Sir Walter Scott came for the fishing. From here it is real walking country – to the summit of the Cheviot (it is boggy and disappointing when you get there) or, from further down the valley, through the hills and around Yeavering Bell.

It is worth the climb up to the 1,182-foot (360m) summit of Yeavering Bell to appreciate the view and the remains of Northumberland's most spectacular Iron Age fortress, with its massive rubble wall, which was once 10 feet (3m) thick. Part of it has been reconstructed to show what it was like then.

More than 130 timber buildings – the largest 42 feet (13m) across – occupied the 13.5-acre (5.5ha) site. Below the hill King Edwin's palace, Ad Gefrin, once stood. It was mentioned by Bede and discovered by excavation in the 1950s – a monument by the road marks the place. St Paulinus baptised local people in the River Glen to the north in AD 627,

and probably preached in Ad Gefrin's most unusual feature, a wooden theatre like an open-air university lecture hall.

The narrow Breamish Valley is one of the greatest joys of the National Park, and Ingram, sited on the Park border, is a fine gateway to it. The small village church (with its large Georgian rectory) is actually more interesting inside than its frowning exterior might suggest – bits of it may be pre-Norman – but most visitors come to Ingram for the scenery. There are car parks and picnic sites along the valley both east and west of the village, and a comprehensive Visitor Centre that holds discoveries from archaeological digs in the Cheviots.

Excellent walking from the village can take you right up to the Scottish border – and beyond. There are Iron Age hill-forts and deserted medieval villages in the valley, too – look out for the earthworks as you walk, especially if the sun is low. Linhope Spout, 3 miles (4.8km) west of Ingram, is one of the county's best waterfalls, reached by a path from Linhope beside the river.

The Simonside Hills, easily reached from Rothbury, contrast with the rounded summits of the Cheviots. They have crags and bogs, and much of the area is heavily planted with conifer forest. There are fine views from many of the summits – try the panorama from Dove Crag for a marvellous taste.

The western edge of the National Park is, if anything, wilder than the east. You can get a taste of the landscape by taking a walk around Tarset Burn. The southern edge of the Park is bounded by well-preserved parts of Hadrian's Wall.

OTTERBURN MAP REF NY8893

Otterburn has always had its place in military history, ever since the Battle of Otterburn, on 19 August 1388, brought together Harry Hotspur, son of the Earl of Northumberland, and Earl Douglas, who commanded a Scots raiding party. Versions of the battle – and opinions about where it actually happened – vary, but most people agree that it was fought by moonlight, that the Scots raiders beat Hotspur in a daring manoeuvre, that Douglas was killed and Hotspur was captured, to be ransomed later. Many of the dead were buried at Elsdon church. The Percy Cross, in a plantation located northwest of the village, is traditionally said to be where Douglas died. Modern soldiers have practised firing on the Otterburn Ranges to the north since 1911. Today they use the latest infantry weapons, artillery and helicopter. There is public access on certain days along rights of way and roads, but not when the red flags fly. Check locally (or call Range Control on 01830 520569) and don't stray or pick anything up.

At Otterburn Mill, originally built in the 18th century, you can buy fine tweeds and woollens.

ROTHBURY MAP REF NU0501/NU0803

One of the main tourist centres of Northumberland, Rothbury, the capital of Coquetdale, is an attractive town, with stone buildings spreading outwards from an irregularly shaped green and a medieval bridge over the River Coquet.

The town suffered from William Wallace's army in the 13th century, and proclaimed the Old Pretender as James III in the 18th, but since the 19th century it has developed as a holiday centre.

The parish church suffers from its Victorian restoration, which destroyed a Saxon tower and left very little of the rest, but it is worth visiting for a glimpse of the font – its bowl dates from 1664, but stands on part of the 9th-century Rothbury Cross, decorated with vigorous Celtic-inspired designs.

East of Rothbury the Coquet rushes through a narrow gorge at The Thrum – you can reach it by a footpath from the bridge. In places no more than 5 feet (1.5m) wide, the river has scoured the sandstone here into contorted shapes; it also powers Thrum Mill's undershot waterwheel. West of Rothbury, near the

■ Insight

THE MODERN MAGICIAN

William Armstrong, born in Newcastle in 1810, began his scientific career while fishing on the River Coquet. He became interested in hydraulics after watching an inefficient waterwheel, and went on to found an engineering works at Elswick on the Tyne making hydraulic cranes and lifts. After the Crimean War he invented the breech-loaded Armstrong Gun, and armour plating for warships. Despite his fortune and peerage he remained a quiet and humble man, fishing the Coquet with his old friends, experimenting and inventing, giving Cragside not only lamps made by his friend, electrical pioneer Swan, but also hydraulic lifts and kitchen spit, telephones between the rooms and electric gongs. Cragside was also the first house in the world to be lit entirely by electric light and visitors can see the lakes that fed the hydroelectric plant in the Power House and the ingenious timber flume, canal and pipeway that brought water to them.

tiny and picturesque village of Holystone, is the atmospheric Lady's Well, a stone-lined pool amid trees, where St Paulinus is alleged – probably wrongly – to have converted and baptised 3,000 locals in AD 627. An 18th-century statue of the saint stands beside the well.

Cragside (National Trust), east of Rothbury, is one of Northumberland's major tourist attractions and can be very busy in high season, but with more than 900 acres (360ha) of country park and gardens, it is usually easy to find a quiet corner. Built for the 1st Lord Armstrong by the architect Norman Shaw, it is a fantastic Victorian creation, a cross between an English manor house and a Bavarian schloss. It hangs over the wooded gorge of Debdon Burn in a sea of trees and its interior is full of heavy, late-Victorian atmosphere, though parts are quite dark and cramped. Spectacular exceptions include the fine library and the drawing room, with its huge alabaster fireplace.

WALLINGTON MAP REF NZ0284

Wallington is a place of history and historians. A medieval castle here was owned by the Fenwicks until 1684 – the last was Sir John, executed for plotting to assassinate William III; his horse, White Sorrel, was taken by the king, who was thrown and killed after it stumbled over a hidden mole hill. Parts of the castle still survive in the cellars of the present plain, square house, built in 1688 and altered around 1745. These changes transformed the inside with a new grand staircase and wonderfully delicate plasterwork, most elaborate in

the high Saloon, where Reynolds' portrait of Sir Walter hangs, and wall cabinets display part of Wallington's famous china collection. In addition, there is fine Chippendale and Sheraton furniture, 18th-century needlework and a fascinating collection of dolls' houses.

The Trevelyans were at Wallington for almost 200 years and one of the family married the sister of historian Lord Macaulay, whose library is now here. Lord Macaulay's great nephew was another historian, George Macaulay Trevelyan; it was his brother who gave Wallington to the National Trust in 1941.

Wallington shone brightest in the 19th century, when Sir Walter Trevelyan and his wife Pauline entertained writers, scientists and artists – Swinburne, the poet from nearby Capheaton, and the painter Millais among them. It was at Ruskin's suggestion that the courtyard was roofed, creating an attractive Italianate central hall with two levels of open arches. Murals of Northumbrian history by William Bell Scott include *The Descent of the Danes*, with Pauline as a woman crying during a Danish raid, and *The Building of Hadrian's Wall*, with Newcastle's town clerk as a centurion, but best of all is Iron and Steel, showing the modern industries of Newcastle.

The stables are almost as grand as the house, with a big central clocktower originally designed as a chapel. The grounds are delightful. They include a beautiful walled garden with a little pavilion and a terrace overlooking lawns and an ornamental stream with banks of flowers – this is one of the National Trust's prettiest gardens.

Elsdon, Heart of Reiver Country

For hundreds of years in the Middle Ages, Elsdon was at the centre of some of the most lawless land in England. It was the capital of the remote Middle March – one of three Marches, or protective areas, set up in 1249 to protect the border lands. The chief threat to the area was from the reivers or mosstroopers – bands of marauders, mostly from north of the border, who carried out raids on local farms, setting crops alight, destroying homesteads and, above all, stealing cattle, sheep and horses. Such was the seriousness of these raids that they influenced the subsequent design of the village. Its wide green, more than 7 acres (2.8ha) in area, was used to pen in animals during a raid, and the entrances to the village were shut off.

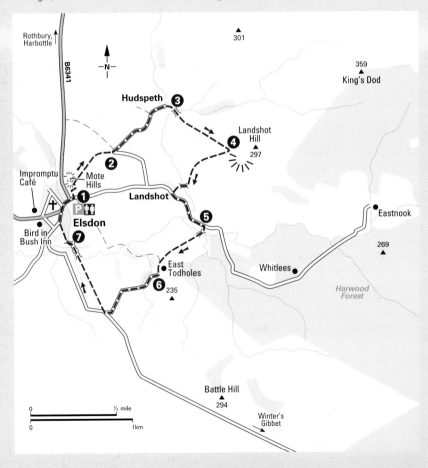

Route Directions

1 Walk away from car park, passing the village hall and toilets on the right. Go through a gateway and climb up the lane past the Mote Hills. Pass the house and cross gravel to a gate. Cross the small field and go through the next gate, then head half right to go through a gate near some trees. Follow the path up a sunken lane, then along the field-edge to reach a gate.

2 Go through the gate and turn left over a cattle grid. Follow the metalled lane through farm buildings and down to a row of cottages. Opposite them, turn right in front of a barn, cross a stream and go through a gate.

3 Go through the field with a bank on your left and, at the top of the rise, bear left across the bank, making for a gate in a crossing wire fence. After the gate, bear half left crossing several ditches to the left-hand end of a crossing wall.

4 Turn right and follow the wall downhill. Go through a gateway in a crossing wall, and continue to follow the wall on your left to reach a waymarked post. Turn right, cross a small bridge, then go

uphill to a gate and ladder stile on the left, before a building. This is a signposted permissive route leaving the right of way. Cross the stile to join a road and turn left. Cross a cattle grid, then a bridge to reach a second cattle grid.

5 Cross the cattle grid, then immediately turn right, signed 'East Todholes'. Cross the stream and go through a gate, then cross a second stream. Follow the wall on your left-hand side to a ladder stile by pine trees. After the stile, bear half left to go round the right-hand side of East Todholes farm and cross a stile on to a lane.

6 Follow the lane past the next farm and up the hill to join a road. Turn right and, in a short distance, cross a stile over the fence on your right. Head half left, down the field to reach an old wall. Follow this downhill towards Elsdon, bending right, then left at a fence to go over a stile. After another stile, bear right to a footbridge, then left to another. The path eventually brings you to a larger footbridge near the village.

7 Cross the footbridge, then turn right to a stile beside a gate. Go up the track between

some houses to a road that takes you to the green. Bear right, along the edge of the green, go over the bridge and back to the village hall at the start of the walk.

Route facts

DISTANCE/TIME
4 miles (6.4km) 1hr45

MAP OS Explorer OL42 Kielder Water & Forest

START Elsdon, by bridge on Rothbury Road, grid ref: NY 937932

TRACKS Field paths and tracks

GETTING TO THE START
The village of Elsdon lies on the B6341 between Otterburn and Rothbury, just inside Northumberland National Park. On entering the village follow the signs to the car park just by the river bridge.

THE PUB Bird in Bush Inn, Elsdon. Tel: 01830 520804

TOURIST INFORMATION CENTRES

Bellingham
Fountain Cottage, Main Street. Tel: 01434 220616

Otterburn
Otterburn Mill.
Tel: 01830 520093

Rothbury
National Park Centre (seasonal).
Tel: 01669 620887

Wooler
The Cheviot Centre,
12 Padgepool Place.
(seasonal)
Tel: 01668 282123

NORTHUMBERLAND NATIONAL PARK CENTRES

Northumberland National Park Headquarters
Eastburn, South Park, Hexham.
Tel: 01434 605555; www.northumberlandnational park.org.uk

Ingram
Visitor Centre (seasonal).
Tel: 01665 578890

Rothbury
Church House, Church Street (seasonal).
Tel: 01669 620887

Northumbrian Water Visitor Centres
Leaplish Waterside Park,
Tel: 01434 251294
Tower Knowe, Kielder Water.
Tel: 0845 155 0236

Kielder Castle.
Tel: 01434 250209;
www.visitkielder.ciom

NATIONAL PARK INFORMATION POINTS

Elsdon
Impromptu Café.
Tel: 01830 520389

Falstone
Falstone Tea Rooms.
Tel: 01434 240459

Kielder
Kielder Garage.
Tel: 01434 250260

Milfield
Milfield Café.
Tel: 01668 216323

Otterburn
The Border Reiver.
Tel: 01830 520682

Wooler
Brands, 43 High Street.
Tel: 01668 281413

OTHER INFORMATION

Otterburn Ranges.
Tel: 0191 239 4201
or 0191 239 4227

PLACES OF INTEREST

Bellingham Heritage Centre
Station Yard,
Woodburn Road.
Tel: 01434 220050

Black Middens Bastle House
Bellingham. Free. www.english-heritage.org.uk

Brinkburn Priory
Longframlington.
Tel: 01665 570628;
www.english-heritage.org.uk

Chipchase Castle
Tel: 01434 630083

Cragside
Rothbury.
Tel: 01669 620333;
www.nationaltrust.org.uk

Kirkharle Courtyard
Kirkwhelpington.
Tel: 01830 540362;
www.kirkharlecourtyard.net

Kirknewton College Valley
Permits to drive beyond Hethpool in advance (personal callers or SAE) from Sale and Partners, 18–20 Glendale Road, Wooler. Tel: 01668 281611. Free.

Wallington House Walled Garden and Grounds
Tel: 01670 773967;
www.nationaltrust.org.uk

FOR CHILDREN

Kielder Water Bird of Prey Centre
Tel: 01434 250400;
www.kwbopc.com
Free.

Otterburn Hall (YMCA)
Tel: 01830 520663;
www.otterburnhall.com
Forest walks, nature trails, rare breeds and gardens.
Free.

SHOPPING

LOCAL SPECIALITIES
Art gallery
Coquetdale Arts Centre,
Rothbury. Tel: 01669 621557;
www.coquetdale.org.uk

Pottery
Westfield Farm Pottery and
Gallery, Thropton, Rothbury.
Tel: 01669 640263
Textiles
Otterburn Mill.
Tel: 01830 520225

■ SPORTS & ACTIVITIES
ANGLING
Fly
Kielder Water Visitor Centre.
Tel: 01434 251000. Permits
from Leaplish Waterside
Park or Tower Knowe
Visitor Centre.
North Tyne River: Tyne
Angling Passport from
Tyne Rivers Trust.
Tel: 01434 611817
BOAT HIRE/TRIPS
Kielder
Kielder Water Cruises.
Tel: 0870 240 3549
From Tower Knowe or
Leaplish. Telephone in
advance. Leaplish Waterside
Park. Tel: 081434 351000
CYCLE HIRE
Kielder
Purple Mountain Bike Centre,
Kielder Castle.
Tel: 01434 250532;
www.purplemountain.co.uk
The Bike Place, Station
Garage, Keilder.
Tel: 01434 250457;
www.thebikeplace.co.uk
Wooler
Haugh Head Garage.
Tel: 01668 281316

HORSE-RIDING
Kirkwhelpington
Little Harle Stables.
Tel: 01830 540334;
www.henriplag.co.uk
Otterburn
Redesdale Riding Centre,
Soppitt Farm.
Tel: 01830 520217; www.
redesdaleridingcentre.co.uk
**COUNTRY PARKS, FORESTS
& NATURE RESERVES**
Bolam Lake Country Park.
Breamish Valley.
Harthope Valley, near Wooler.
Harwood Forest, near
Rothbury.
Holystone Burn Nature
Reserve, near Alwinton.
Thrunton Wood, Callaly.
ORIENTEERING
Kielder
Tel: 01434 250209
WATERSPORTS
Kielder Water
Tel: 01484 250294
**CYCLE ROUTES & LONG-
DISTANCE FOOTPATHS**
Pennine Cycleway
A 355-mile (571km) ride from
Derbyshire to Berwick.
www.pennine-cycleway.co.uk
Pennine Way
A 270-mile (434km) path from
Kirk Yetholm in the Scottish
Borders to Edale in
Derbyshire.
www.nationaltrail.co.uk
Reivers Cycle Route
A 187-mile (300km) ride from
Tynemouth into the Scottish

borders and Whitehaven.
www.rievers-route.co.uk
St Cuthbert's Way
A 62-mile (100km) path from
Melrose to Lindisfarne. www.
stcuthbertsway.fsnet.co.uk

■ ANNUAL EVENTS
& CUSTOMS
Alwinton
Border Shepherds' Show,
mid-Oct.
Bellingham
Bellingham Show, late Aug.
Brinkburn
Summer Music Festival, Jul.
Falstone
Border Shepherds' Show,
mid-Aug.
Forestburngate
County Fair. Aug.
Harbottle
Harbottle Show, Sep (1st Sat).
Kielder Castle
Kielder Forest Festival,
early Aug.
Otterburn
Otterburn Festival, Jul.
Rochester
Upper Redesdale Show, Sep.
Rothbury
Traditional Music Festival,
mid-Jul.
Thropton
Thropton Show, Sep.
Whalton
Baal Fire, 4 Jul.
Whittingham
Whittingham Show, Aug.
Wooler
Glendale Show, late Aug.

CRAGSIDE

Tea Rooms

Harley's Tea Rooms

**Bridge Street,
Rothbury NE65 7SE
Tel: 01669 620240**

In the heart of the bustling village of Rothbury, this is a traditional family-run café housed inside an old stone building. Harley's can provide you with a full afternoon tea, as well as light snacks and full meals – all of them home-made and tasty. Closed Wednesday and Thursday.

Laundry Coffee House

**Kirkharle Courtyard,
Kirkharle Hall,
Kirkwhelpington, Newcastle
upon Tyne NE19 2PE
Tel: 01830 540362; www.
kirkharlecourtyard.co.uk**

One of Britain's most famous garden designers, Lancelot 'Capability' Brown, was born in Kirkharle. The Courtyard is adapted from the old farm buildings of Kirkharle Hall, and is home to a wide variety of craftspeople. The relaxing Laundry Court Coffee House serves home-made cakes and light lunches, using seasonal, local ingredients.

The Otterburn Tower

**Otterburn NE19 1NS
Tel: 01830 520620;
www.otterburntower.com**

Otterburn Tower is a hotel in a battlemented castle that dates back to the Middle Ages and is now a luxurious place to stay. You can take a traditional afternoon tea in the Garden Room, in the panelled dining room or, in good weather, on the terrace or the lawn. Afterwards, walk it off in the 32 acres (13ha) of pretty grounds that include a stretch of the River Rede and, at the right time of year, a bluebell wood.

Pubs

The Anglers Arms

**Weldon Bridge,
Longframlington NE65 8AX
Tel: 01665 520271; www.
anglersarms.fsnet.co.uk**

If you've ever longed to enjoy the luxury of eating in a Pullman carriage, head for the Angler's Arms. You can sample the delights of its impressive restaurant menu either in its special carriage or, more conventionally, in the bar. Border lamb and local salmon feature, and you can also try Northumberland sausage washed down with a selection of real ales.

Bird in Bush

**Elsdon NE19 1AA
Tel: 01830 520804**

The Bird in Bush occupies a corner of Elsdon's wide, triangular green. A traditional Northumberland pub, it provides real ales and excellent, wholesome, home-cooked food in its restaurant and from the bar. The pub is an IT hub, providing the area with broadband access.

The Cheviot Hotel

**Bellingham NE48 2AU
Tel: 01434 220696;
www.thecheviothotel.co.uk**

Bellingham is a magnet for visitors, and the Cheviot Hotel provides a great place to relax, either to enjoy a quiet drink in the bar or to eat in the restaurant. Always using locally sourced ingredients, the hotel's menu includes traditional dishes as well as sandwiches, tasty snacks and a children's menu.

The Pheasant Inn

**Stannersburn NE48 1DD
Tel: 01434 240382;
www.thepheasantinn.com**

Once a traditional and historic Northumberland farmhouse, which for 250 years had a bar as a sideline, the Pheasant is now a warm, cosy pub with photographs of generations of local farmers, miners and smiths around the walls. You can drink a pint of Timothy Taylor's or sample one of many whiskies in the bar, and eat great food either there or in the restaurant.

Along Hadrian's Wall

INTRODUCTION

From Wallsend near the mouth of the Tyne to Bowness on the Solway Firth, Hadrian's Wall swept across the North, 'to separate the Romans from the barbarians' wrote the Emperor's Roman biographer. Much of the Wall, a World Heritage Site, and its forts can still be traced – follow the 84-mile (135km) Hadrian's Wall Path National Trail. It gives a sense of the history of Britain, which later fortifications and the towns along its most impressive sections enhance. The finest stretches of Hadrian's Wall are built on the dramatic dolerite outcrops of the Great Whin Sill, formed 295 million years ago when molten rock forced its way through the earth's crust. This chapter is arranged geographically, east to west, rather than alphabetically.

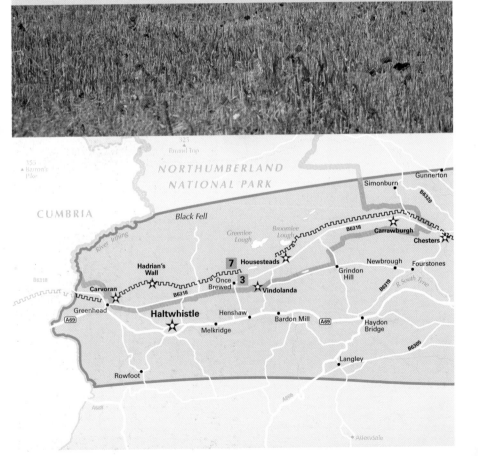

HADRIAN'S WALL

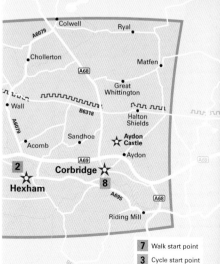

Colwell
Ryal
A6079
Chollerton
Matfen
A68
Great
Whittington
Wall
B6318
Halton
Shields
A6079
Sandhoe
Aydon
Castle
Acomb
A69
Aydon
2
Corbridge
8
Hexham
A695
A68
Riding Mill

7 Walk start point
3 Cycle start point
2 Tour start point

GREAT WHIN SILL

Unmissable attractions

Take in the classic view of Hadrian's Wall from the top of Highshield Crags...explore the remains of the Roman granary at Corbridge...sit in silent meditation in the Saxon crypt at Hexham Abbey...visit the museum at Chesters, once known as Cilurnum fort, to find out about a soldier's life on the Wall...climb the reconstruction of the Roman Wall at Vindolanda...find out about the Roman Army at the Roman Army Museum... walk as much of the Wall as you can...explore the intricacies of Roman plumbing in the latrines at Housesteads.

1 Vindolanda
Finds at the extensive remains of this Roman settlement and barracks have revealed much about the daily lives of soldiers and their families.

2 Bellister Castle, Haltwhistle
Haltwhistle is a pleasant town that makes an excellent base for exploration of the area, although it is well worth spending time here, too.

3 Aydon Castle
Originally a manor house, Aydon was fortified after attacks by the Scots. It has been restored to its early appearance.

4 Hexham
The priory, begun in AD 674, is the result of several centuries of building work.

5 Hadrian's Wall
The survival of sections of this wall is testament to the engineering and construction skills of the Romans who built it.

HADRIAN'S WALL

Around AD 80 the Romans constructed a road – Stanegate – south of the Great Whin Sill. It went from Corbridge, where Dere Street crossed the River Tyne, to Carlisle. Guarded by forts, it was not originally a frontier, for Roman troops were active far into Scotland. But in about AD 100 Emperor Trajan withdrew to the Stanegate, building new forts and watchtowers on the Whin Sill. Trajan's successor, Hadrian, visiting in AD 122, ordered the construction of a wall which would be the limit of the empire and would offer protection from the tribes in the north that resisted Roman invasion.

Running 80 Roman miles – 73 modern miles (117.5km) – the Wall was built of local sandstone and ran between the Tyne and the Irthing; further west turf was used, later replaced by stone. It began 10 Roman feet – 9.5 feet (3m) – wide, later reduced to 8 feet (2.4m), or sometimes 6 feet (1.8m), to speed up the work. The vallum, a high-banked ditch south of the Wall to control civilians at the frontier, was another modification.

No one knows exactly how high the Wall once was – probably around 21 feet (6.4m). For some of its life it was painted with whitewash. There were regular crossing points, for the Wall was never meant to be an impenetrable barrier. Instead, it gave the Romans control over journeys in the area. The barbarians could pass into the empire, but only to approved markets, unarmed and with a military escort. Later, in more troubled times, some of the gates were blocked.

When Hadrian died in AD 138, the new emperor, Antoninus Pius, abandoned the Wall, pushed into Scotland and built the Antonine Wall (of turf rather than stone) from the Forth to the Clyde. But the troops retreated to the Whin Sill in AD 160, when a new route – the Military Way – was built between the Wall and the vallum to improve access.

The tribes north of the Wall were kept in check much of the time, though occasionally there were rebellious outbreaks. By the beginning of the 4th century there was a new menace – the Picts – and successive emperors tried to deal with them. By around AD 407 the empire was breaking up; at this time the British army chose its own emperor, Constantine III, who went off to win Rome, leaving Britain undefended. The auxiliaries at the Wall drifted away, and it became a quarry for local farmers. Hadrian's part in the Wall's construction was forgotten until 1840, and it has only been in the 20th century that the site has gained legal protection.

■ Insight

BUILDING THE WALL

Although Hadrian ordered the Wall, it was built under the supervision of Nepos, Governor of Britain. Construction took eight years and the work was done by soldiers from three legions – the 2nd, based in Caerleon; the 6th, in York; and the 20th, in Chester. They had engineers, surveyors, masons and carpenters – some may have worked in Germany. As work progressed, other soldiers, including auxiliaries, helped, and there may have been locally conscripted labour, too. The cost would have largely been accounted for by the soldiers' normal pay – indeed, it is suggested that the project was devised partly to keep them occupied.

Along Hadrian's Wall

Roman Emperor, Hadrian, ordered the building of a great Wall in AD 122 to repel the Picts and Britons. It was planned to span the countryside between the River Irthing at Thirlwall and Newcastle, but added a turf wall that would extend to the west coast at Bowness on the Solway Firth. After the Romans left Britain the Wall fell into decay and its masonry was used to build churches, farmhouses and field walls.

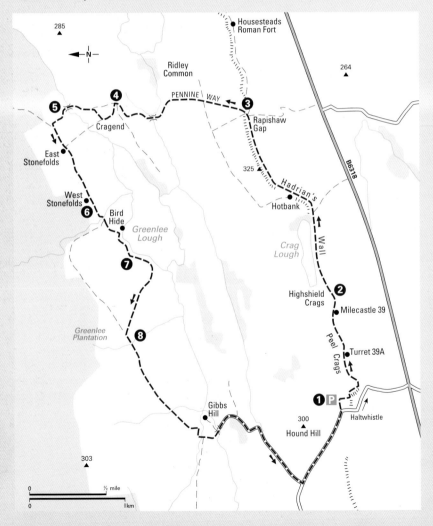

Route Directions

1 From the car park descend to a grassy depression beneath Peel Crags. The path arcs left and climbs back to the ridge in a series of steps then follows the cliff tops past Turret 39A and Milecastle 39.

2 There's another dip, then a climb to Highshield Crags, which overlook Crag Lough. Beyond the lake the footpath climbs past Hotbank farm.

3 At the next dip, Rapishaw Gap, turn left over the ladder stile and follow the faint but waymarked Pennine Way route across undulating moorland. The first stile lies in the far right corner of a large rushy enclosure. A clear cart track develops beyond a dyke and climbs to a ridge on Ridley Common where you turn half left to descend a grassy ramp.

4 The path slowly arcs right to meet and cross a fenced cart track at Cragend. Here a clear grass track zig-zags down to a moorland depression with Greenlee Lough in full view to your left. At the bottom the ground can be marshy and the path becomes indistinct in places. A waymark points a sharp right turn but the path loses itself on the bank above it. Head north here, keeping the farmhouse of East Stonefolds at ten to the hour. The next stile lies in a kink in the cross wall.

5 Beyond this, turn half left to traverse a field before going over a ladder stile and turning left along the farm track, which passes through East Stonefolds. The track ends at West Stonefolds. Walk through the farmyard, heeding the plea from the residents not to intrude too much on their privacy.

6 Past the house continue, with a wall to the left, along a grassy ride, and go over a step stile to reach a signposted junction of routes. Go straight ahead on the permissive path signposted to the Greenlee Lough Bird Hide. The path follows a fence down to the lake. Ignore the stile unless you want to go to the hide itself, but instead continue alongside the fence.

7 Go over the next stile and cross wetlands north of the lake on a duckboard path, which soon swings right to a gate. Beyond this continue on the path, climbing north-west, guided by waymarker posts to the farm track by the clearfelled stumps of the Greenlee Plantation.

8 Turn left along the track and follow it past Gibbs Hill farm. Past the farmhouse a tarmac lane leads back towards the wall. Turn left at the T-junction to return to the car park.

Route facts

DISTANCE/TIME
8 miles (12.9km) 4h

MAP OS Explorer OL43 Hadrian's Wall

START Steel Rigg (pay) car park, grid ref: NY 750677

TRACKS Mainly well-walked National Trails, 16 stiles

GETTING TO THE START
Steel Rigg car park is situated just off the B6318, northeast of Haltwhistle. At the Once Brewed Visitor Centre, turn off the main road and continue through Once Brewed until you reach the car park on the right.

THE PUB The Milecastle Inn, Military Road, nr Haltwhistle. Tel: 01434 321372; www.milecastle-inn.co.uk

❶ Take care not to damage the Wall by walking on it

AYDON CASTLE MAP REF NY9966

Set in a curve of the Cor Burn just north of Corbridge, Aydon Castle is really a very early fortified manor house, built at the end of the 13th century and given its battlements in 1305. Where it was most vulnerable, to the north side, it has an irregular outer bailey, and behind that a small, open courtyard, with the living quarters to one side. Unusually for its early date, there was no keep. Instead there was a hall and a solar with a fine fireplace and some beautifully detailed windows – don't miss the bearded face staring out from above the northern one. Look out, too, for the garderobes – medieval toilets – to be found at the southeast corner of the south range.

Within the walls there was an orchard, so conditions must have been comfortable for this unsettled border country. Despite this it had its times of excitement, being captured by the Scots in 1315, and by English rebels in 1317. In the less fraught 17th century it became a farmhouse – which helped to preserve its main features.

At Halton, 0.75 mile (1.2km) north, you can get a glimpse of Halton Tower (not open), a 14th-century pele with a wing of 1696, and visit the chapel next door. This may be Saxon in origin – it was certainly here in Norman times – and has a wonderfully simple interior, its white-painted walls contrasting with the massive wooden beams of the roof.

CORBRIDGE MAP REF NY9964

The first Roman fort at Corbridge – Corstopitum – was built around AD 90, more than 30 years before Hadrian's Wall, to guard the bridge where Dere Street crossed the Tyne. The Stanegate, built slightly earlier by Agricola's troops, also crosses the fort on its way into Carlisle. As a vastly important junction, Corstopitum had a succession of forts – the one we see today is the fourth, built about AD 140 as the Romans occupied Scotland. It was an important military headquarters, depot and supply base, even after the Romans finally gave up on Scotland towards the end of the 2nd century. By degrees it changed into a town – the most northerly in the Roman Empire – much of which is still buried, though its stones are found in many Corbridge and Hexham buildings.

The excellent museum is full of finds from the site, including inscriptions and some small, often personal objects. The recommended tour takes you first of all past the granaries, perhaps the most memorable part of the fort, and the best preserved in Britain, with floors of stone slabs on low walls.

The square courtyard to the north of the main street (part of Stanegate) was never finished and no one is quite sure what it was. Opposite are the military compounds, where you can trace the workshops and officers' houses before descending into the former strongroom to see where soldiers and locals worshipped both Roman and local gods.

The town, once Northumbria's capital, suffered from invasion by Danes and Scots. Not surprisingly, there are two defensive pele towers in Corbridge. One, at the end of Main Street, dates from the 13th century. It was converted into a house in about 1675.

The other, the Vicar's Pele, is made from Roman stones and was probably put up in the 14th century. Sitting in the churchyard and little altered over the centuries, it remains one of the best peles to be found in the north.

St Andrew's Church, too, uses some Roman stones – between the tower and the nave is a whole Roman archway. The tower's lower parts were probably built before AD 786, and there is more Saxon work in the walls, as well as a Norman doorway and a 13th-century chancel. Lots of stone cross slabs are built into the walls and floors, and part of the chancel floor is a medieval altar stone.

CHESTERS MAP REF NY9170

Where Hadrian's Wall crossed the North Tyne, the Romans built a wooden bridge guarded by Cilurnum fort, now called Chesters. Cavalry were stationed here – no remains of stables have been ever positively identified, but you can see the barrack block. The officers had larger rooms, at the river end of the block. In the centre of the fort, the headquarters were where the commanding officer sat on a raised platform to dispense justice. The rooms behind were used by clerks and the standard bearers, who also looked after the accounts and pay. A stone staircase leads into the vaulted strongroom, which still had its iron-sheathed oak door when excavated in the early 19th century. Both the well-preserved east gate and the west gate have short sections of the Wall attached.

Near the river was the garrison's bathhouse. You can trace its main chambers – the changing room, with

■ Visit

FOUNTAIN LION

Pride of place in the museum at Corstopitum goes to the Corbridge Lion. A finely carved, spirited beast with a bushy mane, it is depicted attacking a stag. It is thought that the lion may have started its life on a tomb, but was later moved to ornament the great fountain in the town. You can still see the fountain's large stone tank, which was fed by an aqueduct, between the granaries and the courtyard building. The tank's edges were worn down over centuries as metal blades were sharpened against the stone.

■ Insight

MILECASTLES

At every Roman mile along the wall was a milecastle, like a tiny fort. It had a gate in its southern wall, and one to the north through the Wall itself, so that travellers could be checked as they passed through it. Most milecastles had barracks for eight men – though a couple of them held 32.

niches probably for clothes, the hot dry room, like a sauna, hot steam rooms, hot and cold baths, as well as the latrine, draining to the river. Furnaces and underfloor heating must have made this a popular place in the camp.

Near by are remains of the bridge, but they are better preserved over on the opposite bank, reached by a footpath from the bridge at Chollerford. In the river you can see an original pier, which carried the wooden pedestrians' bridge, as well as a later stone bridge built in about AD 206 to carry vehicles; two of its three piers can still be seen when the river is low.

Romans and Countryfolk of Corbridge

Corbridge is a picturesque little town, with Georgian stone cottages, antique shops and old inns cuddled up to square-towered St Andrew's Church, built in the Saxon era and with a Roman archway borrowed from the older settlement. Before going down to the River Tyne and the magnificent 17th-century bridge, the route passes Town Barns, where author Catherine Cookson lived in the 1970s. We take a short riverside ramble now, before climbing out of the valley, traversing pastures scattered with woods, and strolling along hedge-lined country lanes. You arrive at Prospect Hill, with its pristine cottages and farmhouses.

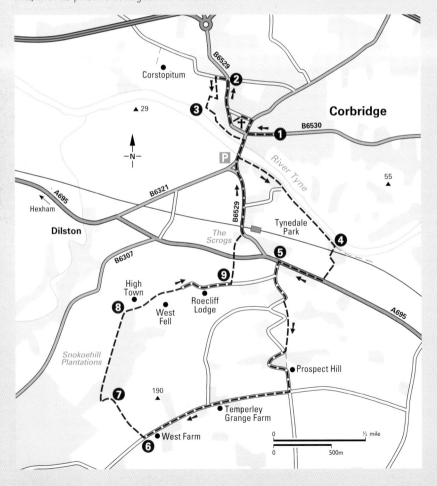

Route Directions

1 The walk begins at Low Hall Pele on the eastern end of Main Street. Head west down Main Street before turning right up Princes Street. At the town hall turn left along Hill Street, then, just before the church, turn left up the narrow street to pass the Vicar's Pele. Turn right at the Market Place and head north up Watling Street, then Stagshaw Road, which is staggered to the left beyond the Wheatsheaf Inn.

2 Go left along Trinity Terrace then left again along a footpath, signed 'West Green'. This leads past Catherine Cookson's old house, Town Barns, to the Georgian house of Orchard Vale, where you turn right, then left along a lane to the river.

3 Turn left along Carelgate, then follow the riverside path to the town bridge. Go over the bridge, then follow the south banks of the Tyne on an unsurfaced track that passes the cricket ground at Tynedale Park before mounting a grassy embankment running parallel to the river.

4 Turn right up some steps, go over a ladder stile, then cross the railway tracks (with care). Another stile and some more steps lead the path through a wood and across a field to meet the A695 where you turn right – there's a footpath on the nearside.

5 Just beyond some cottages, turn left up a country lane, which zig-zags up Prospect Hill. Just after the first bend leave the lane for a southbound path that climbs fields. Just short of some woods the path meets a track where you turn right for a few paces to rejoin the lane. Follow this up to reach a crossroads at the top of the hill, where you turn right.

6 After passing Temperley Grange and West farms leave the road for a path on the right that follows first the right-hand side, then the left-hand side of a dry-stone wall across high fields and down to the Snokoehill Plantations.

7 Go through a gate to enter the wood, then turn left along a track running along the top edge. The track doubles back to the right, soon to follow the bottom edge of the woods.

8 Turn right beyond a gate above High Town farm and follow the track, which becomes tarred beyond West Fell.

Route facts

DISTANCE/TIME
6 miles (9.7km) 3h30

MAP OS Explorer OL43 Hadrian's Wall

START Low Hall Pele on the eastern end of Main Street, grid ref: NY 992642

TRACKS Village streets, riverside and farm paths and lanes, 8 stiles

GETTING TO THE START
Corbridge lies between the A69 and the A695, 3 miles (4.8km) east of Hexham. Main Street is in the south of the town and can be accessed by taking the B6529 (Stagshaw Road) from the north and driving through the town, or via the B6321 from the south and taking the first right turning after the river bridge.

THE PUB The Angel, Main Street, Corbridge. Tel: 01434 632119

9 Beyond Roecliff Lodge a path on the left crosses a field to reach the A695 road. Across the other side of the road the path continues and enters a copse known as The Scrogs, before joining the B6529 by Corbridge Railway Station. Follow this over the bridge and back into Corbridge itself.

Three Dales

A spectacular drive that takes you to the valleys of the Tyne, Wear and Tees and across some of England's wildest and most remote moorland. Much of the route is within the officially designated North Pennines Area of Outstanding Natural Beauty. Note: Some of the route passes over unfenced, high moorland. You should not attempt this drive in bad weather or when visibility is low.

Route Directions

Hexham is a good town to explore on foot, with its attractive Victorian shop-fronts and fine houses.

1 From the centre of Hexham take the B6305 west towards Allendale turning left at the traffic lights by the Fox Inn. Follow the main road, signed 'Allendale', to Catton. Go through Allendale town. Allendale's centre has an attractive square surrounded by stone houses.

2 Continue down the valley of the River East Allen for 7.5 miles (12.1km) through spread-out Sinderhope and on into Allenheads, once an important lead-mining centre. After driving 1.5 miles (2.4km) beyond the village, cross the County Durham border and then descend into Weardale. The B6295 joins the A689 as you reach Cowshill. At the junction you can divert from the main route by turning right for 2.5 miles (4km) to visit Killhope Wheel and the Lead Mining Centre.

A discovery trail leads visitors through the site, devoted to the local lead mining industry.

3 On the main route, turn left to go through Cowshill and Ireshopeburn and into the centre of St John's Chapel, with its 18th-century church and the only Town Hall in a Durham village. Turn right up a narrow entry, Harthope Road, signed 'Langdon Beck'. The unclassified road eventually goes over a cattle grid and climbs steeply on to Harthope Moor. This is one of the highest public roads in England, attaining an altitude of 2,057ft (627m).
The road is marked by tall poles, indicating the route when covered by snow. Do not attempt this route in bad weather or limited visibility.

4 Follow the road for 5 miles (8km), to descend, with wide views of the valley, into Teesdale. At the junction with the B6277 turn left, signed 'Langdon Beck, Middleton'. After half a mile (800m) a

road right leads to Cow Green Reservoir and Cauldron Snout. Continue along the B6277 for 3 miles (4.8km) to reach the spectacular High Force waterfall.
One of the highest single-drop waterfalls in England, this is where the Tees plunges over Great Whin Sill.

5 In 1.5 miles (2.4km) is Bowlees Visitor Centre, and then the road enters the former lead-mining centre, Middleton-in-Teesdale. Immediately after crossing the bridge into Middleton turn sharp left, up a steep hill signed 'Stanhope'. After half a mile (800m) turn right, again signed 'Stanhope'. After 4.5 miles (7.2km) pass over a cattle grid, round a sharp right-hand bend and turn left immediately, then left again on to the B6278.
The road goes over moorland with spectacular views.

6 After 8.5 miles (13.7km), descend into Weardale. Just before the river the road

bends left and then right over
a bridge to join the A689.
Turn right into the centre of
Stanhope and turn left, signed
'B6278 Edmundbyers', just
beside the Grey Bull public
house. Go up the steep hill
through Crawleyside and
after 2.5 miles (4km), where
the main road goes slightly
right, continue ahead on an
unclassified road, signed
'Blanchland'. Follow this road
for 5.5 miles (8.8km) across
open moorland and descend
into the valley of Beldon Burn
at Baybridge. Go over the
bridge, crossing back into
Northumberland, and follow
the road into Blanchland.
The honey-coloured, mainly
18th-century houses in the
centre of Blanchland are set
around two informal squares
separated by an archway of
the monastic gatehouse.

7 In the village take the
road straight ahead beside
the abbey tower, signposted
'Corbridge, Hexham'. As the
road ascends there are views
over Derwent Reservoir. The
road passes through Slaley
Forest and descends to the
very narrow Linnels Bridge
over Devil's Water, and
2 miles (3.2km) further takes
you back into the centre of
Hexham town.

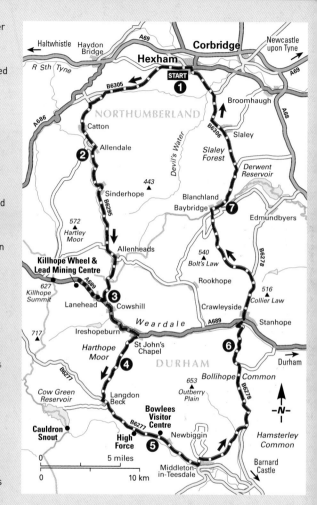

HEXHAM MAP REF NY9364

St Etheldreda made a gift of Hexham manor to her spiritual adviser, Wilfrid, for supporting her against her husband King Egfrith. Wilfrid built the priory – it was never an abbey – in about AD 674. His biography, written around AD 700, describes 'the very deep foundations, the crypts of beautifully finished stone, the great building supported by different columns, walls of wonderful height and length. We have never heard of anything like it this side of the Alps'. Wilfrid's crypt, reached from the new nave built in 1907, was built of Roman stones from Corstopitum (Corbridge), many still with carvings or inscriptions. The 7th-century plasterwork is still rock-hard.

The rest of the priory is impressive, too, especially the early 13th-century choir, the north transept with fine lancet windows and, in the south transept, the Night Stair for the Augustinian canons to descend from their dormitory for night prayers. Look out for the nearby Roman tombstone of standard-bearer Flavius. The stalls in the choir have nicely carved misericords, while Prior Leschman's Chantry contains carvings of unlikely subjects like a bagpiper, a fox preaching to geese and a lady combing her hair.

The priory was kept apart from the town by a row of houses set towards the market place, with its stone-columned Shambles. In 1761 the famous Riot Act was read here to leadminers who were protesting against conscription. Be sure to make time to visit 14th-century Moot Hall, a miniature castle with an archway tunnelling through it, which now houses the Art Gallery. Through the arch, in

■ Insight

SAXON SEAT

In the chancel of Hexham Abbey is one of its treasures, the stone chair called Wilfrid's Seat or the Frith Stool – frith means 'sanctuary', and those who sat on it claimed the protection of the Church. Dating from the time St Wilfrid built the church, the chair had a place of honour in the Saxon building, and is ornamented with plait and knot patterns. The great crack that splits across it was due not to violence or natural disaster, but to the Victorian workmen who dropped it in 1860.

■ Insight

CENTRING ON THE ARTS

Hexham has an annual music festival based at the priory, but for year-round entertainment, the enterprising Queen's Hall Arts Centre opposite is the place to go. Housed in the former town hall (which looks like a French *mairie*), the centre has an intimate 400-seat theatre, with a constant programme of professional and amateur theatre, music and other events; a public library; a gallery and studio, both showing a wide variety of changing exhibitions, and a good restaurant.

Hallgate, is another fearsome tower, the Archbishops' Gaol. Built about 1330, it houses the Border History Museum and Library.

Hexham is a very pleasant town to stroll around, with some fine houses and stunning Victorian shopfronts. The street names, too, have real charm – St Mary's Chare and Priestpopple, for example. Tyne Green is a riverside country park and Hexham Race Course lies to the south of the town.

CARRAWBURGH

MAP REF NY8771

Brocolitia, the fort here at Carrawburgh, remains largely unexcavated, though it is known to have been an afterthought to the Wall, added in around AD 130. The vallum alongside the Wall had to be filled in before Brocolitia could be built, and, unlike the design of earlier forts, it did not project north of the Wall.

Near by are the remains of the most complete Mithraic temple to be found in Britain. Originally an Eastern religion that told of the struggle between light and dark, Mithraism was the most popular religion along the wall, rivalling Christianity, which had by this time become the official religion of Rome. The temple was built low and dark, representing the cave where Mithras slayed the primeval bull and in doing so brought innumerable benefits to mankind. The uninitiated gathered in a small ante-room. Beyond this was the temple, with three altars (those you see

today are replicas) and statues of Mithras's attendants, Cautes, with his torch raised to represent light, and Cautopates, torch down for darkness.

One of the altars shows Mithras as the Unconquered Sun. Above the altars there was once a sculpture of Mithras and the Bull – perhaps destroyed by Christians during the 4th century. The seven Mithraic grades of worshippers; Father, Courier of the Sun, Persian, Lion, Soldier, Bridegroom and Raven, would sit or kneel on low wattle and wooden platforms as the mysteries, which included a symbolic meal of bread and water, took place.

The original altars, as well as other artefacts, can be seen in the Great North Museum in Newcastle upon Tyne; there is also a full-scale reconstruction of the temple there, highly coloured as it was when it was built.

HOUSESTEADS MAP REF NY7869

Housesteads – Roman Vercovicium – is the most visited fort on Hadrian's Wall due to its spectacular site, impressive remains and access to one of the best parts of the wall. Consequently it can be crowded on summer weekends.

To get an idea of the main features, and see some of its treasures, visit the museum first, then climb to the remains of town buildings by the South Gate. These buildings may have been shops or taverns – they still show the grooves that once held shutters.

The gate itself was rebuilt as a bastle in the Middle Ages for a family of horse-thieves. Through it, to the right, you can visit the communal latrines,

■ Insight

BRITANNIA DESOLATA

Coventina's Well, a powerful spring beside the fort at Carrawburgh, was dedicated to a Celtic water goddess, whom the Romans were happy to include in their beliefs. Protected by a shrine, the spring attracted votive coin-throwers – more than 16,000 coins were excavated in 1876, mostly small change, but with some silver and gold too, as well as other objects including a bronze model of a Scottie dog. There were brass coins, too, struck when the Emperor Antoninus Pius put down the North after local rebellion in AD 155; they show defeated Britannia with bowed head and lowered banner, the picture of submission.

where 12 soldiers could sit, rinsing their sponges in the water channels.

Housesteads followed the usual fort pattern, with the headquarters in the centre and the commanding officer's house south of it. You can also see the remains of the hospital, complete with operating theatre, and the granaries. The North Gate has huge foundations on the crag above Knag Burn – the fort protected this vulnerable point. A classic wall view is from the northeast corner of the fort, over the burn.

Walk along the wall westwards from Housesteads to Milecastle 37 – the views are wonderful – and on, if you can, to Steel Rigg, worth the effort to see how the fearsome military structures of Rome have been absorbed into the Northumbrian landscape.

VINDOLANDA MAP REF NY7867

Agricola had a turf fort at Vindolanda in the AD 80s to guard the Stanegate, and part of the paved road, as well as a Roman milestone, can still be seen here. Another fort was built before Hadrian's time, and when the Wall was put up, the fort was rebuilt in stone, then almost totally rebuilt 100 years later, with its usual rectangular shape. The layout of the headquarters and parts of the gates are clearly visible.

Vindolanda also has the biggest civilian settlement that can be seen on the wall. Visit the mansio (an inn for travellers) with its bathhouse, and the large 'corridor' house, part of which was a butcher's shop. Other buildings, long, thin 'strip houses', had their narrow ends to the street to avoid high taxes. The

■ Visit

CLAYTON'S COLLECTION

Without John Clayton (1792–1890) there would be much less of Hadrian's Wall. A lawyer by training, Clayton managed a successful practice. To prevent the gradual destruction of the Wall by people taking stones for building material, he bought long stretches of the Wall and several of the forts, including Housesteads. In addition, he owned and landscaped the Chesters estate and fort. Clayton was active as an archaeologist, laying open to view many Roman remains, and collecting objects from them.

The fascinating museum at Chesters is a memorial to him. Among its treasures are statues of a reclining river god, from the commanding officer's bathhouse, and the (now headless) goddess Juno Dolichena. Notice, too, the corn-measure from Carvoran, which erred generously towards the Romans.

■ Insight

ROMANS AND RAILWAYS

Did railway engineer George Stephenson, who came from Wylam only 20 miles (32km) away, study Roman cart tracks at Housesteads' East Gate? It was once the fort's main entrance, but one of its two arches was soon blocked, and the guardroom used as a coalhouse. So the other side took all the traffic, and over the centuries the passage of carts wore grooves in its stone threshold. They are 4 feet 8.5 inches (1.4m) apart – standard railway gauge today, thanks, at least in part, to Stephenson.

Alas for romance, the East Gate was still unexcavated in Stephenson's day. But the link remains, for farm carts retained this axle span when he began his engineering career. Despite Brunel's attempts at an 8-foot (2.5m) gauge, Stephenson's decision to use traditions more than 1,500 years old won the day.

town bathhouse was frequented by women and children as well as men – hairpins and a child's sandal were found in the drains. You can still see some of the pink waterproof plaster that lined the walls and floors.

Children visiting Vindolanda usually make straight for the reconstructions of sections of Hadrian's Wall, based on archaeological evidence. The Turf Wall shows what the original, Cumbrian, part of the wall was like before it was rebuilt in stone. Here it has a timber gateway, as may once have been found at the milecastles. More impressive is the

■ Insight

VINDOLANDA TABLETS
One of the best-known tablets records an invitation to a birthday celebration. It was sent by Claudia Severa, wife of the commander of the fort at Briga, to Sulpicia Lepidina, wife of Cerialis, who was the commander at Vindolanda. She wrote a message warmly inviting her friend to come and help her make sure that the day of her birthday was one of celebration.

■ Activity

A RAILWAY NAME?
Haltwhistle's intriguing name might suggest a link with the railway – indeed, this was once an important junction on the main east–west line to Carlisle, where passengers could change for a scenic Pennine route to Alston, long since closed. But the name has been around much longer. It was Hautwisel in 1240, and seems to mean 'the place where the streams meet by the hill' – although other suggestions are 'the high place by the crescent of water' and 'high boundary'. All of them fit with Haltwhistle's geography.

Stone Wall, nearly 23 feet (7m) high, with battlements, turret and ditch.

Vindolanda's waterlogged soil has helped to preserve many details of daily life – the museum shows some of them, including leather shoes, textiles and ornaments. There is also a replica of a Roman kitchen. Most important are the wooden writing tablets, with gossip, party invitations, letters requesting new underwear, and accounts of food stores, bringing the Romans and their neighbours vividly to life.

HALTWHISTLE MAP REF NY7064
Haltwhistle Burn flows into the South Tyne east of the town of Haltwhistle, and there are pleasant walks alongside the burn up to Hadrian's Wall. Haltwhistle is also a good place from which to explore the north Pennines. But don't neglect the attractive town centre, its stone streets radiating from the market place giving it a slightly stern, Scottish air. Some of its Victorian station buildings, including the stationmaster's house, waiting room and ticket office, date from as early as 1838. The Red Lion Inn is based on a defensive tower, probably of the 17th century, when Haltwhistle was still at the mercy of Scottish raiders. It was under the protection of the powerful Ridley family (still big landowners in Northumbria); the tomb of John Ridley, brother-in-law to Nicholas Ridley, the Protestant martyr burned at the stake in 1555, is in Holy Cross Church.

The church is one of the best in Northumberland, at least on the inside – its exterior is rather unprepossessing, though the setting is pleasant. It is mostly Early English in style, with long, thin lancet windows, and was carefully restored in 1870, when the wonderful stained glass, made by William Morris's company, was put in the east windows. Haltwhistle was once a thriving centre of industry (there are still manufacturing plants in and around the town), and by the burn you can see the remains of woollen mills, collieries and brickworks.

Great Chesters fort – Aesica – is 2 miles (3.2km) north and was built around AD 128, after the wall, to guard the Caw Gap. Not much is left, though a blocked gateway can be seen, and you can trace the remains of an aqueduct that supplied the fort with water.

CARVORAN MAP REF NY6667

Magnis fort at Carvoran was built before Hadrian's Wall, to guard the junction of the Stanegate and the Maiden Way, running from the South Tyne to the Eden Valley in Cumbria. You can still make out the main shape, but the only stones still visible are part of the northwest tower. Adjoining the fort is the exciting Roman Army Museum, with finds from Magnis and other sites along the Wall, and a large-scale model of the fort. Push-button displays provide instant access to specific details so that visitors can select information. The museum also brings to life the daily existence of the soldier on the Wall, with full-size figures decked out in uniform and weapons used by the legionnaires and auxiliaries. Find out how much they were paid, what they ate, how they trained – and how they overcame the boredom of life spent waiting at the edge of the Empire.

QUIS CUSTODIET?

Hadrian's Wall wasn't guarded by shivering Italian legionnaires, but mostly by auxiliary troops, recruited from Britain or elsewhere in the northern Empire. They were divided into mixed infantry and cavalry regiments of 500 men, though there were some of 1,000. Their officers were often inexperienced aristocrats who were serving briefly before returning to civilian life and relying on experienced subordinate soldiers. Infantry units were divided into centuries – oddly, with 80 men – and cavalry into troops of 32, led by professional soldiers – one centurion is known to have served 58 years. They spent their time patrolling the wall or training. Centurions were not allowed to marry, but often had unofficial liaisons in the civilian towns at the fort walls.

East of Carvoran, the wall runs over the Nine Nicks of Thirlwall, which were once nine gaps in the Whin Sill, but have been reduced over time to five by intense quarrying. Turret 45A was probably a signal post in use while the Wall was being constructed – its stones are not keyed into the structure. Just to the west, there is a fine stretch of the vallum, and further beyond this lies 14th-century Thirlwall Castle, beside Tipalt Burn. Built, as usual, to defend the castle against the marauding Scots, where there was a gap in the wall, the castle played host to Edward I in 1306, but was largely derelict by 1542. The last inhabitants were known to have left in the 18th century, although the ghost of a dwarf is supposed to remain, tirelessly guarding a gold table.

Around Hadrian's Wall and the Stanegate

This cycle route takes you along the finest section of Hadrian's Wall, past two Roman forts and along an ancient Roman road. Hadrian's Wall became a World Heritage Site in 1987 and in 2005 the name was changed to the Frontiers of the Roman Empire WHS. The site was extended to include the remains of the Roman frontier between the rivers Rhine and Danube. The Roman Empire had conquered as far as Mons Graupius in Northern Scotland by AD 83 but unable to hold their gains the Romans gradually withdrew to a line stretching from the Solway Firth to the Tyne. There they built a chain of forts along the road known since medieval times as the Stanegate. When the emperor Hadrian came to power he decided to consolidate the frontiers of his empire and in AD 122 had a wall built close to the line of Stanegate to 'separate the Romans from the barbarians' in the north – in other words, the Scots – who refused to accept Roman dominion.

The ride takes in Housesteads fort, the most visited on the Wall, so in order to avoid the crowds it might be best not to plan your cycle ride for a weekend falling in high summer. Along the route the views of the Wall and the surrounding countryside are spectacular and the temptation to dismount and explore will be strong.

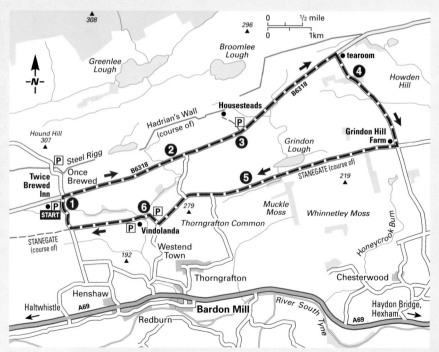

Route Directions

1 Exit the car park and turn left. At a T-junction turn right on to the B6318. (A turn almost immediately to the left heads uphill to reach a car park at Steel Rigg, where a footpath leads walkers along one of the finest sections of Hadrian's Wall. See Walk 7.)

2 Continue along the B6318. This is a straight, undulating road with a superb view of the Wall on your left. After cycling approximately 2 miles (3.2km) pass a turn-off signed for Bardon Mill on your right and in another 0.5 mile (800m) pass the car park for Housesteads fort.

3 Housesteads is the most complete Roman fort in Britain and you may want to spend some time exploring here. Afterwards continue along the road for another 1.7 miles (2.7km) then turn right at a sign for Haydon Bridge. The building on the corner here has a tea room and is built on the site of a Roman signal station.

4 Head along this narrow lane cycling downhill at first, followed by a short, energetic pull up to the top of the next hill. Just past Grindon Hill Farm take a right turn at the crossroads on to 'Cycle Route 72', heading towards Bardon Mill. This is the line of the Stanegate, an important Roman road that ran from Corbridge to Carlisle.

5 Keep ahead on 'Cycle Route 72' with a grand view of the Wall on your right and over Thorngrafton Common on your left. There is a great view of Housesteads and, further on, Vindolanda. After a downhill section make a right turn, still continuing on 'Cycle Route 72', following signs for Vindolanda.

6 Head downhill to reach the museum entrance. Pass by the entrance then continue uphill, passing the top car park and a thatched cottage before reaching a T-junction. Turn right on to the 'Pennine Cycle Route 68' and keep on it to reach the start.

Route facts

DISTANCE/TIME 12 miles (19.3km) 2h

MAP OS Explorer OL43 Hadrian's Wall

START National Park Visitor Centre car park (fee payable) at Once Brewed, grid ref: NY752668

TRACKS Roads and country lanes

CYCLE HIRE Eden's Lawn Cycle Hire, Haltwhistle. Tel: 01434 320443

GETTING TO THE START The National Park Visitor Centre car park is just off the B6318 at Once Brewed (off the A69 east of Haltwhistle).

THE PUB Twice Brewed Inn, Once Brewed, Bardon Mill (on the B6318 just along from the Visitor Centre). Tel: 01434 344534

❶ Moderate inclines, no off-road sections. Suitable for children and riders of all abilities.

■ TOURIST INFORMATION CENTRES

Corbridge
Hill Street (seasonal).
Tel: 01434 632815

Haltwhistle
Railway Station
Tel: 01434 322002

Hexham
Wentworth Car Park.
Tel: 01434 652220

■ NORTHUMBERLAND NATIONAL PARK CENTRES

Headquarters
Eastburn, South Park,
Hexham.
Tel: 01434 605555; www.
northumberlandnationalpark.
org.uk

Once Brewed
Military Road, Bardon Mill.
Tel: 01434 344396 (seasonal).

■ NATIONAL PARK VILLAGE INFORMATION POINTS

Gilsland
Post Office.
Tel: 01697 747211

Langley
The Garden Station.
Tel: 01434 684391 ;
www.thegardenstation.co.uk

■ PLACES OF INTEREST

Aydon Castle
Corbridge.
Tel: 01434 632450;
www.english-heritage.org.uk

The Old Gaol
Hallgate, Hexham.
Tel: 01434 652349;
www.tynedaleheritage.org

Carrawburgh (Mithraic Temple)
On the B6318, 3.75 miles
(6km) west of Chollerford.
www.english-heritage.org.uk
Free.

Chesters Bridge Abutment
On A6079 0.25 mile (400m)
south of Low Brunton.
www.english-heritage.org.uk
Free.

Chesters Roman Fort and Museum
Chollerford.
Tel: 01434 681379;
www.english-heritage.org.uk

Corbridge Gallery
Tourist Information Centre,
Hill Street.
Tel: 01434 632815

Corbridge Roman Site
Tel: 01434 632349;
www.english-heritage.org.uk

Dilston Physic Garden
Dilston Mill House,
Dilston, Corbridge.
Tel: 07879 533875;
www.dilstonphysicgarden.com

Moot Hall
Market Place, Hexham.
Tel: 01434 652351;
www.tynedaleheritage.org

Roman Wall (Housesteads Fort and Museum)
Bardon Mill.
Tel: 01434 344363;
www.english-heritage.org.uk

Vindolanda (Chesterholm)
Bardon Mill. 1.25 miles (2km)
southeast of Twice Brewed.
Tel: 01434 344277;
www.english-heritage.org.uk

Walltown Crags and Turret
On B6318, 1 mile (1.6km)
northeast of Greenhead. Free.

■ FOR CHILDREN

The Old Gaol
Hallgate, Hexham.
Tel: 01434 652135/652349;
www.tynedaleheritage.org

Hadrian's Wall
Many milecastles, turrets and
sections of wall are freely
open. They include Brunton
Turret, 0.25 mile (400m)
south of Low Brunton on
A6079; Sewingshields
Milecastle, 1 mile (1.6km)
east of Housesteads, and
Milecastle 42 near Cawfields,
2 miles (3.2km) north of
Haltwhistle.

Roman Army Museum (Carvoran)
Greenhead.
Tel: 01697 747485
Exciting museum, with a
large-scale model of the fort,
push-button displays,
full-size figures showing
uniform, armour and
weapons of legionnaires.

■ SHOPPING

Haltwhistle
Market, Thu.
Hexham
Main shopping area:
The Shambles. Market, Tue.
Farmers' markets 2nd and
4th Sat of every month.

LOCAL SPECIALITIES
Fine Art
FiFieFoFum
Westside Farm,
Newton, Corbridge.
Tel: 01661 843778;
www.fifiefofum.com
Pottery
Errington Reay, Bardon Mill
Pottery, Bardon Mill.
Tel: 01434 344245;
www.erringtonreay.co.uk
Large salt-glazed pots and
water features.
The Potting Shed, 1–3
Broadgates, Hexham.
Tel: 01434 606811;
www.thepottingshed.co.uk
Terracotta pots for house
and garden.
Stencilling
The Stencil Library,
Stocksfield Hall (off B6309).
Tel: 01661 844844;
www.stencil-library.com
Stencils and accessories.

■ PERFORMING ARTS

Hexham
The Queen's Hall Arts Centre,
Beaumont Street, Hexham.
Tel: 01434 652477;
www.queenshall.co.uk
Theatre, exhibition gallery
and library.

■ SPORTS & ACTIVITIES
ANGLING
Contact Tourist Information
Centres and local fishing
tackle shops.
COUNTRY PARKS
Tyne Green Country Park,
Hexham.
CYCLE HIRE
Hexham
The Bike Shop
16 St Mary's Chare.
Tel: 01434 601032; www.
thebikeshophexham.com
HORSE-RIDING
Bardon Mill
Cragside Stables, Low
Fogrigg, Westwood.
Tel: 01434 344065
Dipton Mill, Hexham.
Plover Hill Riding School,
Burnside.
Tel: 01434 607196
Humshaugh
Sharpley Farm Pony and
Carriage Driving Centre.
Tel: 01434 681239;
www.sharpleyfarm.co.uk

CYCLE ROUTES & LONG-DISTANCE FOOTPATHS
Hadrian's Cycleway
Coast to Coast the Roman
Way. A 174-mile (280km)
ride from the Cumbrian
coast to the North Sea.
www.cycle-routes.org
Hadrian's Wall Path
An 84-mile (135km) walk
from Wallsend to Bowness-
on-Solway.
www.nationaltrail.co.uk

■ ANNUAL EVENTS & CUSTOMS
Corbridge
Northumberland County
Show, Spring Bank
Holiday Mon.
Gilsland
Gilsland Show, early Aug.
Haltwhistle
Walking Festival, Spring
and Autumn.
Hexham
Abbey Festival, mid-Sep.
Folkworks Hexham
Gathering, late May.
Twice Brewed
Roman Wall Show, Jun.

Tea Rooms

St Oswald's Tea Room

St Oswald's Farm Wall,
Hexham NE46 4HB
Tel: 01434 689010

You can take tea virtually on Hadrian's Wall at St Oswald's Tea Room – it's set between the sites of two Wall turrets. A converted and extended stable, the tea room serves quiches, soups, pies and cakes, all home-made, and a wide range of teas.

Mrs Miggins's Coffee House

9 The Granary, St Mary's Wynd, Hexham NE46 3LZ
Tel: 01434 605808

Any resemblance to Mrs Miggins's establishment in the *Blackadder* television series is purely one of name, for this Hexham café has an airy, comfortable look, and serves a wide range of home -cooked food. You are likely to rub shoulders with local people who have popped in to sample the excellent scones.

Vallum Farm Tearoom

Eastwallhouses, Military Road, Newcastle upon Tyne NE18 0LL
Tel: 01434 672652;
www.vallumfarm.com

A modern tea room housed in a pine cabin by Hadrian's Wall, Vallum Farm has an outstanding menu of freshly made produce, all of it from nearby – ask the source of an egg, and they'll know the chicken's name! Try the fruit and cheese scones with strawberry jam and cream, both from producers within shouting distance. There is an ice cream parlour, too.

Pubs

Dipton Mill Inn

Dipton Mill Road, Hexham NE46 1YA
Tel: 01434 606577;
www.diptonmill.co.uk

Dipton Mill Inn is a country pub lying a few miles from Hexham, beside a stream. In the summer you can sit outside in the garden. It offers good bar meals, but its secret is that round the back there is the Hexhamshire microbrewery that produces its own real ale including Devil's Water, Whapweasel and Old Humbug.

General Havelock

Ratcliffe Road,
Haydon Bridge NE47 6ER
Tel: 01434 684376

The garden of the General Havelock, a converted barn, overlooks an idyllic stretch of the River South Tyne. There is an interesting range of ales on tap, and the menu has a number of interesting twists on the usual fare, with local produce used as much as possible. An insider praises the lemon tart!

Milecastle Inn

Military Road, Cawfields,
Nr Haltwhistle NE49 9NN
Tel: 01434 321372;
www.milecastle-inn.co.uk

Only a few hundred yards from one of the best bits of Hadrian's Wall, the stone-built Milecastle Inn has a beamed bar – you can eat here or in the restaurant. Local game is a strong suit of the menu, and people travel miles just to sample one of the speciality pies – try the Poacher's Pie, with beef and venison, or the wild boar and duckling pie.

Twice Brewed Inn

Bardon Mill, Hexham NE47 7AN
Tel: 01434 344534;
www.twicebrewedinn.co.uk

Not far from both the Roman sites at Vindolanda and Housesteads, this inn is a wonderful place to relax from the rigours of marching up and down Hadrian's Wall. In the bar there is always a great selection of real ales, and you can eat well in the bar and the restaurant. Local produce is to the fore. Leave room for the ice creams.

Cities & Saints

The cities of Newcastle, Durham and Sunderland dominate this area and each has its own unique character. Once famous as the industrial centre of the north, the region is much altered from the days of shipbuilding and mining. But even in the bustling cities, fine countryside is never far away.

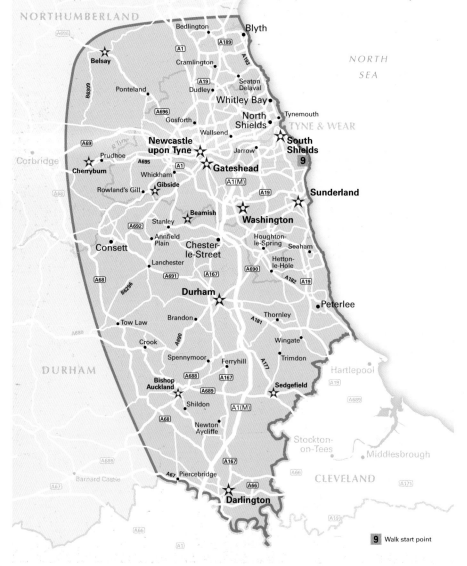

9 Walk start point

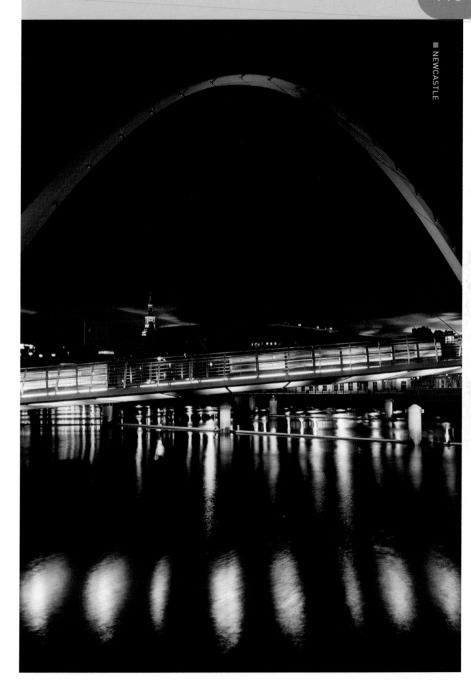

Unmissable attractions

Walk over Newcastle's bridges, from the Tyne Bridge to the Millennium Bridge...sit and contemplate Durham Cathedral's nave...picnic on the banks of the Wear near Prebend's Bridge in Durham...shop at the MetroCentre in Gateshead...enjoy the nightlife on The Quayside in Newcastle...climb the Grey monument in Newcastle ...eat a stottie cake...experience life as it was a century ago at Beamish Museum... cheer on the Magpies, otherwise known as Newcastle United Football Club, at their ground at St James' Park...climb the tower and see the light at Souter Lighthouse ...watch glass being made at the National Glass Centre in Sunderland...marvel at the survival of the Venerable Bede's Saxon church at Jarrow.

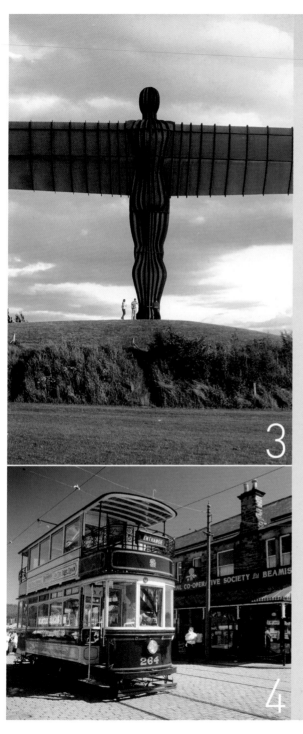

1 South Shields
Souter Lighthouse stands south of the town, a 76-foot (23m) beacon that has been operational since 1871. This distinctive red-and-white striped tower was the first lighthouse to use electricity to emit its powerful life-saving light.

2 Durham
One of Durham's finest buildings, the cathedral sits on the banks of the River Wear. It featured as one of the classrooms in a Harry Potter movie and was voted Britain's favourite building in a recent poll to find the best of British architecture.

3 *Angel of the North*
The landmark steel statue which stands at the entry to Tyneside was designed by sculptor Antony Gormley. The Angel stands 65 feet (20m) high. Almost £600,000 of the funding for the project came from the National Lottery.

4 Beamish
The open-air working museum at Beamish is a major visitor attraction. Many of the buildings have been removed from their original locations and rebuilt here. Visitors can see how their ancestors lived and worked by visiting their actual homes and workplaces. Authentic details as well as the costumed interpreters bring everything vividly to life.

■ Visit

RAILWAY FIRST

Causey Arch, 1 mile (1.6km) northwest of Beamish and built in 1727, claims to be the world's oldest railway arch. At 105 feet (32m) long it was the largest single-span bridge in the world at the time. The surrounding picnic site with displays telling its history.

■ Visit

THE QUARRY GARDEN

If Belsay Hall is austere, even chaste, the Quarry Garden is romantic and voluptuous. Created when the stone was dug for the new Hall, it has secret, winding chasms in the sandstone, and leaf-strewn paths overhung with exotic trees and planted with rampant flowers and shrubs. Laid out by Sir Charles Monck, it is said to be based on gardens in Syracuse. Monck's grandson, Sir Arthur Middleton, carried on the plans and developed the planting elsewhere on the estate, especially on the terrace and parterre. There is a rose terrace and a magnolia garden.

■ Insight

BEWICK'S MEMOIR

'Cherryburn House, the place of my nativity, and which for many years my eyes beheld with cherished delight, is situated on the south side of the Tyne, in the county of Northumberland, a short distance from the river. The house, stables, &c., stand on the west side of a little dean, at the foot of which runs a burn. The dean was embellished with a number of cherry and plum trees... near the House were two large ash trees growing from one root... The cornfields and pastures to the eastward were surrounded with very large oak and ash trees... It was with infinite pleasure that I long beheld the beautiful wild scenery which was there exhibited'.
– A Memoir of Thomas Bewick, written by himself (1828).

BEAMISH MAP REF NZ2253

Watching period drama on television – especially programmes based the novels of Catherine Cookson – will have made many familiar with Beamish, 4 miles (6.4km) northwest of Chester-le-Street. Set in 200 acres (81ha) of beautiful countryside, the North of England Open Air Museum has reconstructed a turn-of-the-century northern town.

Costumed staff welcome visitors to shops stocked with period goods, and serve at the pub and newspaper office, bringing Beamish vividly to life. You can take part in a lesson held in the village school, worship in the Methodist Chapel or explore the mysteries of the Masonic Temple, ride on a tram, catch a train or experience the hard life of the pit village – disasters in the mine sharpening the demanding daily grind. For some, the ultimate horror might be a visit to the old-fashioned dentist. The Home Farm, with its traditional farm animals, used to supply Beamish Hall, once owned by the Shafto family. Amid all the fun of Beamish, don't miss the fine statues of a shepherd and shepherdess standing above the doorway of the village inn.

BELSAY MAP REF NZ0978

The glowing yellow sandstone walls and sturdy battlements of the 14th-century tower-house of the Middleton family remain almost complete. It is as if the structure were still standing ready to repel the marauding Scots who made its construction and fortification necessary in the first place. Even the Great Hall's painted wall decorations, looking just like tapestries, are well preserved.

In 1614 a manor house was added, and this was rebuilt during the 19th century. Now roofless, it was largely abandoned when Sir Charles Monck (originally a Middleton, he changed his name on inheriting the property) built his startling new house near by.

Belsay Hall is Greek in style and is severely plain and symmetrical, each side 100 feet (30.5m) long. The interior of Sir Charles's house – he was his own architect – is even more awe-inspiring. The central hall is two storeys high with a glazed roof, and is surrounded by columns. It is a splendid room, and perfectly proportioned, but the overall effect is rather cold and over-formal.

The other rooms cannot live up to this masterpiece, although they do have fine fireplaces and good views. Only the cavernous cellars are as impressive.

BISHOP AUCKLAND
MAP REF NZ2028

Bishops have lived at Auckland since the 12th century, but Auckland Castle has been their main residence since Durham Castle was given to the University in 1832. Just off the market place is the toy-like 18th-century gatehouse, but it is the bishops' home and its lovely green parkland, freely open to walkers, that draw visitors to this rather dour town.

Entrance to the castle is through a Gothic screen that frames the chapel, built in the 12th century as the Great Hall and converted by Bishop Cosin after 1661. Inside is his typical sumptuous but dark furnishing. Everything – especially the ceiling – is decorated with his badge, a diagonal cross on a diamond. Much of the rest of the castle has a prosperous 18th-century look, especially the State Rooms, including the Throne Room (Durham's bishops still acted like royalty even as late as this). After all this Anglican pomp, it is pleasant to wander in the park, with Bishop Trevor's pretty Gothic deerhouse and the mature, majestic trees.

Even more than the Saxon churches at Jarrow and Monkwearmouth, the church at Escomb, 3 miles (4.8km) northwest of Bishop Auckland, takes us back to the time of Bede. Typically tall and narrow, many of its stones come from the Roman fort at Binchester near by, where you can visit part of the headquarters building and its hypocaust heating system. Escomb church was once larger; you can see the outline of demolished parts indicated in stone. But otherwise only the early Gothic lancet windows, and the three larger Victorian ones, have changed in appearance since well before the Norman Conquest.

CHERRYBURN MAP REF NZ0762

Thomas Bewick, Britain's greatest wood-engraver and a superb naturalist, was born at Cherryburn in 1753. His countryside childhood is celebrated in the lively tailpieces he engraved for his books, especially *A General History of Quadrupeds* and the *History of British Birds*. The farmhouse, home to later Bewicks, now houses an exhibition of his life and works. You can also see the farmyard cottage where he was born, and there is a variety of farm animals around. On demonstration days prints are made in the adjoining barn.

DURHAM CATHEDRAL

DARLINGTON MAP REF NZ2814

The Victorian market hall, with its proud tower, still attracts shoppers to Darlington, for centuries an important market town. Another tower adorns Bank Top Station, a reminder that Darlington's worldwide fame comes from the first passenger railway, the Stockton and Darlington, built by George Stephenson and opened in 1825. The former North Road Station was opened in 1842 and now houses the Head of Steam Museum, the prize exhibit of which is *Locomotion No 1*, the first engine to be used on a public railway. On its maiden trip it hauled a 90-ton train, with Stephenson driving. There are more railway relics at the national Railway Museum's 'Locomotion' museum at nearby Shildon

Fine 18th- and 19th-century houses reflect Darlington's prosperous past, and there are some most impressive public and commercial buildings, too. Engineering works, attracted by the railways, undertook projects throughout the world, including the renowned Sydney Harbour Bridge.

St Cuthbert's, the 12th-century parish church, is one of the best of its date in the north. Hardly altered since Bishop le Puiset founded it about 1192, its tall spire makes a powerful statement.

Piercebridge, 5 miles (8km) west, is an attractive village built over a Roman camp. Dere Street crossed the River Tees here – an early bridge downstream from the village was replaced around AD 100 by another, in use until the 1200s. You can still see its abutments and, it is said, oak piers when the river is low.

DURHAM MAP REF NZ2742

Even without its finest buildings – the great cathedral and castle that dominate its skyline – the city of Durham would be spectacular. The River Wear does a huge loop, in a deep ravine, coming almost to meet itself. From this superb defensive position the city grew over the centuries, down the hill and outwards, but from whichever side you approach – and especially if you arrive at the station by rail – Durham is a magnificent sight.

The city is a place for visiting on foot. Gently climbing from the market place up Saddler Street you will see elegant Georgian houses from one of Durham's most prosperous times interspersed with small specialist shops and several university departments. Owengate leads into Palace Green, dominated by the cathedral's north side and surrounded by fine university buildings, with the castle to your right.

It was in Durham that St Cuthbert's bones finally ended their century-long journey from Holy Island in AD 995, but the present cathedral building, with its three massive towers, dates from 1093. Enter by the north door with its replica sanctuary ring (a 12th-century door-knocker). The original is in the Treasury.

The main effect of the interior is of enormous strength. Huge columns, alternate ones patterned with bold geometric incisions – spirals, zig-zags and diamonds – hold up the earliest Gothic roof anywhere. Not far from the font, with its riotous canopy given in 1663 by Bishop Cosin, a black stone line in the floor shows how far women were allowed into the monastic church. The east wall is dominated by a rose window, and below it is the Neville Screen, made from creamy stone. Beyond this is the 13th-century Chapel of the Nine Altars, with its tall lancet windows, overlooked by St Cuthbert's tomb which has just a simple stone slab. In the choir, the Bishop's throne is the highest in Britain. When the monks tried to build a Lady Chapel near Cuthbert's tomb, it is said that the misogynist saint supernaturally interfered with the work, causing it to be abandoned. Instead, in about 1170, they built a Galilee Chapel at the west end (well away from St Cuthbert), perched precariously over the ravine. The tomb of the Venerable Bede is here.

Off the cloisters, try not to miss the Monks' Dormitory, with its huge wooden roof, and the Treasury, full of fine silver,

■ Insight

THE PRINCE-BISHOPS

For centuries – until 1836 – the Bishops of Durham were a law unto themselves. William the Conqueror created them Earls – later they became the Prince-Bishops – to protect this remote part of his kingdom. Like some German bishops, but uniquely in Britain, they held absolute power in their very extensive lands. Bishops had their own parliament, they made the law, they minted coins and controlled the army. It was they, not the king, who granted permission for the nobles of the north to build castles, and even the king had to ask permission to enter the Palatinate. The defence of the bishopric is still symbolised by the ceremonial presentation of a fearsome knife – the 13th-century Conyers Falchion, now in the Cathedral Treasury – as a new Bishop enters the diocese for the first time at Croft on the Tees.

gorgeous pre-Conquest embroidery and manuscripts, and relics of St Cuthbert, including his cross and coffin. To get the classic cathedral view, go to Prebends' Bridge, reached from South Bailey.

The castle, begun in 1072, now houses University College, and its 18th-century gatehouse has a Norman core, as does the massive keep, which was rebuilt in 1840. Bishop Cosin's ornate Black Staircase leads from the medieval Great Hall to the 18th-century State Rooms and the College Chapel. The real highlight of a tour around the castle, though, is a visit to the splendid Norman gallery and the Norman chapel.

College buildings cluster in the streets around the castle and cathedral, though the university has expanded into several modern buildings to the south of the city. Elsewhere, the city becomes more work-a-day, though the churches – particularly St Oswald's, near the elegant Kingsgate Bridge – are worth exploring. The Heritage Centre at St Mary-le-Bow, North Bailey, vividly tells the history of Durham, while Durham University Oriental Museum, off Elvet Hill Road, is full of wonderful Chinese porcelain and jade. The Durham Light Infantry Museum reflects the military past of the regiment and the city, and houses the art gallery.

A good way to see the best the city has to offer is to take this 2.5-mile (4km) walk. Start in the Market Place, and from the statue of Lord Londonderry on his horse, walk along Silver Street to descend to Framwellgate Bridge, built by Bishop Flambard in about 1128 and rebuilt after a flood in 1401. Immediately at the end of the bridge turn left down the steps by the Coach and Eight pub to reach the riverbank, going ahead with the castle and cathedral across the river. Now walk behind the riverside buildings to Prebends' Bridge, begun in 1772 with funds from the Canons (Prebendaries) of the cathedral. Do not cross the bridge, but continue alongside the river. On the opposite bank you will see the charming Grecian-style Count's House.

Walk along the riverside path until it ascends into St Oswald's churchyard. Turn left into Church Street and at the end of the buildings, go left over the modern Kingsgate Bridge, then up the steps at the end and into Bow Lane. At the top, turn left along North Bailey (if the cathedral is closed, turn right here and then take the first left on to Palace Green). After about 100 yards (91m) go right through the 16th-century archway leading to the delightfully informal little square called The College. Follow the wall on the right and turn right at its end to go through a tunnel into the cathedral cloister. Go left and then right, around the cloister and into the cathedral.

Leave the cathedral by the south door and keep ahead towards the castle. At the end of the first building go left, signed Museum of Archaeology, past the house where J M Falkner, the author of *Moonfleet* and *The Lost Stradivarius*, lived during his retirement. He was Honorary Librarian of the cathedral. Falkner died in 1932 and there is a plaque dedicated to his memory in the cloister. Continue down to a crossing path, turn left and follow the main path downhill to the east end of Prebends' Bridge.

Turn sharp right along the riverbank, past the Museum of Archaeology and up the steps on to Silver Street. Turn right and after a few yards take another right turn to go through a narrow opening into Moatside Lane. Follow the passage to emerge in Saddler Street, and then turn left into the Market Place.

GATESHEAD MAP REF NZ2562

Antony Gormley's huge steel figure of *The Angel of the North* stands on the edge of Gateshead (junction of the A1 and A167). It symbolises the resurgence of the town, which was long dominated by its northern neighbour, Newcastle.

The other herald of regeneration is the Millennium Bridge, with its 'blinking eye' mechanism that tilts to let ships pass beneath it. This new bridge gives pedestrians and cyclists easy passage between the Newcastle Quayside and the redeveloped Gateshead Quays.

Dominating the south bank is the Baltic Centre for Contemporary Art, developed in a former flour mill and housing art galleries, restaurants, live performance spaces, a cinema and a library. Beside it are found the gleaming curves of the Norman Foster-designed Sage Centre, with performance venues, educational areas, studios, bars and cafés. Elsewhere in Gateshead is the huge MetroCentre – more than just a shopper's paradise – and the Gateshead International Stadium. The Derwent Walk Country Park enfolds woodland and water-meadows, while at Bill Quay Community Farm you can admire Gloucester Old Spot and Saddleback pigs, Longhorn cattle and Jacob sheep.

GIBSIDE MAP REF NZ1758

The Gibside estate was the brainchild of George Bowes, an ancestor of the late Queen Mother. The great house and most of the buildings are in ruins but the chapel, framed by a shady avenue of Turkey oaks, is carefully tended by the National Trust. Designed by Paine in 1760, it was only completed in 1812. The interior is reached through a columned entrance beneath a central dome and six fine urns. It is not as ornate as Paine intended – he wanted more elaborate plasterwork and statues. The three-decker pulpit, with a cover like a pagoda roof, dominates the interior, while the small altar seems to be an afterthought.

NEWCASTLE UPON TYNE
MAP REF NZ2464

It is said that Queen Victoria kept the blinds down as she entered Newcastle on the royal train. She missed a place of vibrant energy, then and now, and one of the friendliest of northern cities, though she would probably have disapproved of today's rich nightlife. Her train passed, unseeing, the keep of the New Castle itself – new in 1080 and founded by the Conqueror's illegitimate son, Robert Curthose. It was rebuilt 100 years later during the reign of Henry II, and there are fine views of the city from the roof.

The Victorian railway builders cut ruthlessly through the castle ward, so the medieval entrance, the Black Gate, is now separated from the keep. A picturesque brick house of about 1620 perches on top of its 13th-century lower floors. The railway goes into Central Station, a masterpiece of Newcastle architect John Dobson. The huge curved train shed, supported by slender iron columns, was much imitated. From here you can connect with the Metro system, still the most convenient way of getting around Newcastle. The hub of the Metro system is Monument Station, just by the column to Earl Grey, the 19th-century parliamentary reformer.

To the west is the modern Eldon Square Shopping Centre, while to the south is Grey Street, one of the best streets in Europe. Lined with elegant, columned buildings, the street curves satisfyingly as it descends towards the Tyne. Near the top the lively Theatre Royal, northern home of the Royal Shakespeare Company and of the National Theatre, adds a punctuation mark with its portico.

Bessie Surtees House, nearer the river, is a survivor from an earlier Newcastle, and has a half-timbered front with a vast array of small-paned windows. From one of them, marked with blue glass, rich Bessie eloped with her poor lover John Scott; he later rose to become Lord Chancellor Eldon.

The river near here is crossed by four of Newcastle's most famous bridges: Robert Stephenson's High Level Bridge was finished in 1849, with twin decks for trains and cars; the Swing Bridge was built 25 years later by Armstrongs and was once driven by their hydraulic engines; the semicircular Tyne Bridge is the bridge that immediately conjures up 'Newcastle' to homesick Geordies all over the world. The Millennium Bridge leaps over the Tyne from Quayside, where a famous Sunday morning market

■ Visit

ARMS AND THE DENE

The wooded valley of Jesmond Dene, formed by meltwater retreating after the last ice age, was developed by Lord Armstrong, arms magnate and local benefactor. His house near by has been demolished, but the walks and bridges laid out for him remain in this unusual park, where swans can be seen on the pools and a waterfall tumbles over rocks. Armstrong used to allow visitors into his park twice a week, on payment of a small fee which helped a local hospital. In 1883 he presented it to Newcastle as a free public park, and it has been much loved and visited ever since.

is held. It is also the departure point for boat trips on the Tyne. The Quayside is also the focus of Newcastle's youth culture, with pubs and clubs jostling with each other in the streets around.

Two church towers dominate this part of Newcastle. Classical All Saints – now deconsecrated – has a fine spire attached to a very unusual elliptical body. The Cathedral of St Nicholas, with its splendid tall crown, was threatened with destruction from Scots' cannon fire during the Civil War, but mercifully the firing ceased when the Mayor decided to fill the cathedral with Scottish prisoners.

Newcastle has more than its fair share of excellent museums to visit. The Great Northern Museum, with its fine Roman artefacts, is the principal museum for Hadrian's Wall, and also houses John Hancock's magnificent collection of birds, as well as geological exhibits, making it one of the finest

collections in the country. Newcastle Discovery tells the city's story. Stunning Victorian paintings can be seen at Laing Art Gallery, including several by local visionary artist John Martin.

Horse-racing at High Gosforth Park, north of the city, is also popular. The Northumberland Plate meeting in June, a valuable 2-mile handicap, is also known as 'The Pitmen's Derby' because all the collieries used to be closed so that the miners could attend.

SEDGEFIELD   MAP REF NZ3528

'Racing from Sedgefield' conjures up images of peaceful, rural England, and though it is near Tyneside and Teesside, the town is just that. The racecourse is on its southwestern edge and has a reputation for having a relaxed, warm and friendly atmosphere. At the heart of the village the church, with its grand 15th-century tower, is surrounded by tall trees and old gravestones, Georgian houses and pantiled cottages. Inside is woodwork – hearty Gothic pinnacles and luscious carving – given by Bishop Cosin's son-in law, rector here from 1667 and later Dean of Durham.

An archway by the Hardwick Arms leads to Hardwick Hall Country Park. Its first owner spent so much on the garden buildings that he couldn't afford to build a house, but now most of them are in ruins, or have vanished altogether. The Country Park's gateway was always a ruin, however, having been deliberately built as such. Now the park is open for birding, pond-dipping, picnicking or just strolling along the boardwalk nature trail through Fen Carr.

SOUTH SHIELDS MAP REF NZ3666

Signs in this area say 'Welcome to Catherine Cookson Country' and visitors can follow the Cookson Trail around South Shields and visit a reconstruction of her childhood home in the museum. Modern South Shields has a real air of prosperity, with its wonderful position at the river mouth and its fine beaches. To the south, the distinctive 76-foot (23m) red-and-white striped tower of the Souter Lighthouse is open to the public.

The Romans built South Shields' Arbeia fort as a supply base for their military campaign against Scotland. On special Roman Days volunteers of the 'Cohors Quinta Gallorum' show how 3rd-century soldiers lived.

To the west is Jarrow, famous for the Crusade of 1936. Led by Jarrow's Labour MP, 'Red' Ellen Wilkinson, malnourished and desperate workers, unemployed since Palmer's Shipyard closed in 1933, marched to London, stirring the nation's sympathy but no Government action, except to cut their unemployment pay for the time spent on the road.

The Venerable Bede lived at Jarrow monastery from AD 682, when he was 12, and wrote his *Ecclesiastical History* here in AD 731. Incredibly, the church he knew – dedicated in April AD 685, as we are told on its dedication stone – still survives and its nave has now become the chancel of the present building. The ruins found to the south of the church are from a later Benedictine monastery. Across the park, the Bede's World Museum contains some finds from the site and has reconstructions of Anglo-Saxon timber buildings.

SUNDERLAND MAP REF NZ3957

The city of Sunderland was once a small port surrounded by much larger and better-established villages, including Bishopwearmouth and Monkwearmouth. Coal transportation and shipbuilding caused its spectacular growth during the 18th and 19th centuries, and though the shipyards no longer cluster around the mouth of the Wear, Sunderland is a bright young city. In the warm weather crowds of people flock to the sands of Roker and Seaburn, north of the river; among varied winter entertainments is the famous pantomime at Sunderland's Empire Theatre, opened in 1907.

A lively and interesting selection of museums can be found in and around the city. Stained glass was first made in Britain at Monkwearmouth, and in the city's National Glass Centre, on the River Wear, the myriad uses of glass today are explained and celebrated. It is on the Glass Trail, which takes visitors to see glassblowing and gives them the chance to buy glassware at factory prices.

At the Museum and Winter Garden in Burdon Road, Sunderland, Lustreware pottery is on display. At Ryhope, south of Sunderland, the Engines Museum is housed inside Victorian buildings; the enormous pumping engines of 1869, usually in steam on Bank Holidays, are always an awesome sight. Across the river is the North East Aircraft Museum.

Not too far away, Hylton Castle, built around 1400, has fine battlements and a resident ghost. Modern arts and crafts are on display at the Reg Vardy Arts Foundation Gallery at Sunderland University, and at the Northern Gallery

for Contemporary Art. From the north end of the Wearmouth Bridge it is but a short walk to reach the Greek-style Monkwearmouth Station Museum, built in 1848 and preserved as it was at the turn of the 20th century. Transport and travel in the early 1900s are recorded here, with a look behind the scenes of the booking offices and guard's van.

The Venerable Bede was born in Wearmouth in AD 673 and when he was seven he entered the new monastery (hence Monkwearmouth) founded by St Benedict Biscop in AD 674. Parts of his church survive – the lower part of the tower and part of the tall, narrow nave is 7th century, the rest of the tower is 9th century, the chancel is from the 1300s and the north aisle from 1874.

WASHINGTON MAP REF NZ3155

American visitors to this Washington will not find a city like their own capital but a New Town, based on 16 village centres, half of them new. Most visitors, however, will make for Washington Old Hall (National Trust), the home of George Washington's ancestors – even though most of the building dates from around ten years after the de Wessyngtons sold up in 1613. The house is furnished in the 17th-century style, with polished oak furniture, pewter plates, and some fine Jacobean panelling. There is, of course, a bust of George Washington, and a family tree that traces his ancestry to King John. Celebrations here perpetuate the American connection by marking Washington's Birthday in February, as well as Independence Day on 4th July and Thanksgiving in the autumn.

Coal from Washington's mines was transported to the River Tyne along the Bowes Railway, which is now preserved at Springwell Village. The world's only standard-gauge, rope-hauled railway, it was begun by George Stephenson in 1826. You can take a ride on a steam-hauled train, follow a historical trail and visit a fascinating exhibition.

The Wildfowl and Wetlands Trust, east of Washington, was founded by Sir Peter Scott. Its 114 acres (45ha) of parkland are home to flamingos, swans, geese and ducks, as well as to flocks of migrating waders and wildfowl. Hides let you see the shyer species and picture windows in the Visitor Centre give wide-ranging views in bad weather.

Each July Washington hosts the two-day Sunderland International Friendship Festival, when kite-makers and -flyers from around the world meet for the UK's biggest event of its kind. This lively event includes street theatre, music and activities for children.

Art-lovers could sample Washington Arts Centre, a converted farm building that houses an exhibition gallery, artist studios and a community theatre.

Dominating the landscape from its hilltop southeast of Washington is the Penshaw Monument, a soot-blackened half-size replica of the Temple of Theseus in Athens. It was built by local subscription as a tribute to the 1st Earl of Durham, 'Radical Jack' Lambton, a great local benefactor who became the first Governor of Canada. Near by is another example of historical copying – the Victoria Viaduct, which is a replica of the Roman bridge at Alcantara in Spain.

Smugglers and the Light of Marsden Bay

This walk takes you along the coast near South Shields, and inland to the Cleadon Hills. You will pass two windmills: the first, in Marsden, is a squat building that retains its sails; the other, higher on the hills, was built in the 1820s, and survived until the end of the century, when it was damaged in a storm. In the Second World War it housed Royal Observer Corps members who scanned the North Sea for enemy aircraft. The red-and-white striped Souter Lighthouse was opened in 1871 to protect ships from the rocks called Whitburn Steel, just off the coast. Originally it was nearly 0.25 mile (400m) from the sea, but erosion has brought the cliff edge much nearer.

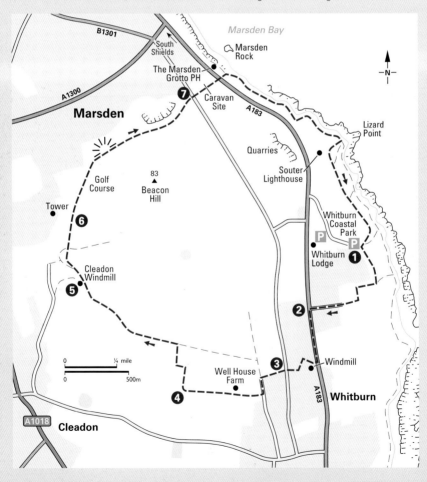

Route Directions

1 Leave the car park at its southern end, following the gravel track toward the houses. The path winds and goes past a sign for Whitburn Point Nature Reserve. Follow the track ahead to go through a gap in a wall and turn right. The path bends right, left and right again to join a road into houses. Go straight ahead to join the main road.

2 Cross the road and turn left. Walk down the road until you reach the windmill. Turn right to enter the grounds of the windmill. Go up the slope on the path, then between houses. Bear left, then turn right to reach a T-junction.

3 Go straight ahead on a path that goes to the right of house No.99. When you reach another road turn left. Just after the first bungalow on the right, turn right along a signed track. Follow the track towards the farm. Go through the farmyard over two stiles and follow the lane beyond, with a hedge to your right. Where it ends, turn right over a stile.

4 Follow the path along the field-edge. Go over another stile, gradually ascending. The path bends left then right, still following the field-edge. Go over another two stiles. The path will bring you to the tower of Cleadon Windmill.

5 Go to the right of the windmill, following the wall on your right. Go right through a kissing gate, then bear slightly right (a brick tower to your left). Go parallel with the wall on your right. Cross a track and go through a wire mesh fence at right angles to the wall. Follow the path through scrubland to emerge by a yellow post by the golf course.

6 Cross the course, following the yellow posts and looking out for golfers. Go over a stone stile and turn right along a signed footpath, following the wall on your right. The path eventually descends beside houses to a road.

7 Cross and take the footpath almost opposite, to the right of a caravan site, heading towards the sea. Carefully cross the busy A183, then turn right, following the sea edge. Marsden Rock is near by, and the Marsden Grotto to your left as you cross the road. Follow the coast as it bends left to Lizard Point. After a visit to Souter Lighthouse, continue ahead on a path

slightly inland from the coast, which returns you to the start.

Route facts

DISTANCE/TIME
5.5 miles (8.8km) 2h

MAP OS Explorer 316 Newcastle upon Tyne

START Whitburn Coastal Park car park, grid ref: NZ412635

TRACKS Roads, tracks, field and coastal paths

GETTING TO THE START
Whitburn is on the A183 coast road just north of Sunderland. The entrance to the coastal park is to the north of Whitburn town on the coastal side of the road. Turn right after entering and follow the road down to the car park at the end. If this National Trust car park is closed, use the municipal car park next to the Whitburn Lodge pub.

THE PUB The Marsden Grotto, Coast Road, Marsden.
Tel: 0191 455 6060

■ TOURIST INFORMATION CENTRES

Darlington
13 Horsemarket.
Tel: 01325 388666

Durham
2 Millennium Place.
Tel: 0191 384 3720

Newcastle upon Tyne
Guildhall, Quayside.
Tel: 0191 277 8000

■ PLACES OF INTEREST

Bede's World
Church Bank, Jarrow.
Tel: 0191 489 2106;
www.bedesworld.co.uk

Binchester Roman Fort
Bishop Auckland.
Tel: 01388 663089;
www.durham.gov.uk

Cherryburn: Thomas Bewick Birthplace Museum
Tel: 01661 843276;
www.nationaltrust.org.uk

Crook Hall and Gardens
Durham City.
Tel: 0191 384 8028;
www.crookhallgardens.co.uk

Finchale Priory
Durham. Tel: 0191 386 3828;
www.english-heritage.co.uk

Gibside Park and Chapel
Rowlands Gill.
Tel: 01207 541820; www.
nationaltrust.org.uk

Great North Museum
Barras Bridge, Newcastle.
Tel: 0191 222 6765;
www.museums.org.uk/
greatnorthmuseum

National Glass Centre
Liberty Way, Sunderland.
Tel: 0191 515 5555;
www.nationalglasscentre.com

Seaton Delaval Hall
Seaton Sluice, Whitley Bay.
Tel: 0191 237 1493;
www.nationaltrust.org.uk

Shipley Art Gallery
Gateshead.Tel: 0191 477
1495; www.twmuseums.org.
uk/shipley. Free.

Souter Lighthouse
Sunderland.
Tel: 0191 529 3161;
www.nationaltrust.org.uk

Tanfield Railway
Sunniside, Gateshead.
Tel: 0845 468 4938;
www.tanfield-railway.co.uk

Tynemouth Castle and Priory
Tel: 0191 257 1090;
www.english-heritage.co.uk

Wildfowl and Wetlands Trust
Washington Wetland Centre.
Tel: 0191 416 5454;
www.wwt.org.uk/visit-us/
washington

■ FOR CHILDREN

Blue Reef Aquarium
Grand Parade, Tynemouth.
Tel: 0191 258 1031;
www.bluereefaquarium.co.uk

Discovery Museum
Blandford Square, Newcastle.
Tel: 0191 232 6789;
www.twmuseums.org.uk/
discovery. Free.

Seven Stories
Centre for Children's Books,

30 Lime Street, Newcastle.
Tel: 0845 271 0777;
www.sevenstories.org.uk

■ SHOPPING

Darlington
Indoor market, Mon-Sat.
Open-air market, Mon, Sat.

Durham
Open-air market, Sat.
Indoor market, Mon–Sat.
www.durhammarkets.co.uk

Gateshead
The MetroCentre.
Tel: 0191 493 0219;
www.metrocentre.uk.com

Newcastle upon Tyne
Grainger Indoor Market,
Mon–Sat.
Quayside market, Sun.
Jesmond, Bridge Market,
weekends.

■ LOCAL SPECIALITIES

Art, Ceramics and Glass
The Biscuit Factory, Stoddart
Street, Newcastle.
Tel: 0191 261 1103;
www.thebiscuitfactory.com

Ceramics
Sedgefield Pottery, Cross
Street, Sedgefield.
Tel: 01740 621998;
www.sedgefieldpottery.co.uk

Crafts
Gateway World Shop,
Market Place, Durham.
Tel: 0191 384 7173;
www.stnics.org.uk

Outdoor Clothing
Barbour Factory Shop,

Simonside, South Shields.
Tel: 0191 428 4707;
www.barbour.com

■ PERFORMING ARTS
Darlington
Civic Theatre, Parkgate
Tel: 01325 486555;
www.darlington.gov.uk
Gateshead
The Sage Gateshead.
Tel: 0191 443 4661;
www.thesagegateshead.org
Newcastle upon Tyne
Theatre Royal, Grey Street.
Tel: 08448 112121;
www.theatreroyal.co.uk
South Shields
The Customs House, Mill
Dam. Tel: 0191 454 1234;
www.customhouse.co.uk
Sunderland
Empire Theatre.
Tel: 0844 847 2499;
www.sunderlandempire.co.uk

■ SPORTS & ACTIVITIES
ANGLING
Witton le Wear.
Tel: 01388 488691;
www.wittoncastlelakes.co.uk
BOAT TRIPS
Durham
Prince Bishop River Cruises,
Elvet Bridge. Tel: 0191 386
9525; www.princebishop.co.uk
Newcastle upon Tyne
River Tyne Cruises, River
Escapes. Tel: 01670
785666/785777;
www.riverescapes.co.uk

COUNTRY PARKS
Allensford Park, Consett.
Derwent Walk, Gateshead.
Herrington Country Park,
Sunderland.
Lambton Castle Park,
Chester-le-Street.
Queen Elizabeth II, Ashington
Watergate Forest Park,
Gateshead.
CYCLE HIRE
Durham
Cycle Force Ltd, 29 Claypath.
Tel: 0191 384 0319
Gateshead
Whickham Thorns Activity
Centre, Market Lane,
Dunston. Tel: 0191 433 5767
Newcastle upon Tyne
Newburn Leisure Centre,
Grange Road, Newburn.
Tel: 0191 264 0014
FOOTBALL
Darlington , Northern Echo,
Darlington Arena. Tel: 0871 855
1883; www.darlington-fc.net
Newcastle United, St James'
Park. Tel: 0844 372 1892;
www.nufc.talent-sport.co.uk
Sunderland, Stadium of Light.
Tel: 0871 911 1974;
www.safc.talent-sport.co.uk
HORSE-RIDING
Crook
Hole In The Wall Riding
School, Chelyn, Church Hill.
Tel: 01388 764835
Durham
Ivesley Equestrian Centre,
Waterhouses.
Tel: 0191 373 4324;

www.ridingholidays-iversley.
co.uk
**CYCLE ROUTES & LONG-
DISTANCE FOOTPATHS**
Bede's Way
A 13-mile (21km) path and
cycle route linking Jarrow
and Wearmouth.
**Consett and Sunderland
Railway Path**
A 26-mile (42km) route.
Durham Coastal Footpath
An 11-mile (18km)
waymarked route from
Seaham to Crimdon.
Three Rivers Cycle Route
A 135-mile (217km) cycle
route linking the Tyne, Wear
and Tees estuaries.

■ ANNUAL EVENTS & CUSTOMS
Durham
Durham Miners' Gala, Jul.
Durham County Show,
mid-Jul.
Newcastle upon Tyne
Newcastle Hoppings, Jun.
Great North Run, autumn.
Winter Festival, Dec.
Tynemouth
Mouth of the Tyne River
Festival, Jul.
International Youth Football
Tournament, Aug.
North Tyneside Kite Festival,
Aug.
Washington
Egg Rolling at Penshaw
Monument, Easter.
Kite Festival, early Jul.

Tea Rooms

The Almshouses

Palace Green,
Durham DH1 3RL
Tel: 0191 386 1054;
www.the-almshouses.co.uk
A tea room with a fantastic view, it hobnobs with Durham Castle on one side and the cathedral on the other. It's a handy place for an afternoon tea or for something more substantial at lunchtime, including vegetarian dishes, soups and generous salads.

The Herb Patch

Brockwell House, Newlands,
Ebchester DH8 9JA
Tel: 01207 562099;
www.herbpatch.fsnet.co.uk
As its name suggests, this is a herb nursery run on organic lines. You can browse the nursery, shop at the farm shop, then relax in the very attractive tea room, where home-made cakes and scones are available, along with fresh soups and light lunches. Many of the dishes are, of course, flavoured with herbs, and herb teas and infusions are available, too.

Rendezvous Café

Dukes Walk,
Whitley Bay NE26 1TP
Tel: 0191 252 5548; www.
rendezvouswhitleybay.com
Enjoy the sea view from the huge windows of this iconic 1930s art deco building, as you enjoy the delicious cream teas, fine pastries and even a typically seaside hot dog! Its been in the same family for more than 50 years, and they've got the formula exactly right for the stunning location. Seasonal opening.

Pubs

Dun Cow

43 Front Street,
Sedgefield TS21 3AT
Tel: 01740 620894
A village pub that has been patronised by an American President and the British and French prime ministers, the Dun Cow is in the heart of Sedgefield. It's a charming building with several different eating areas, where you can dine well – fish is a speciality (try the sea bass in olive oil with roast tomato if it's listed) as well as local specialities.

George Hotel

Piercebridge-on-Tees
DL2 3SW
Tel: 01325 374576;
www.georgeontees.co.uk
The George, where the original 'Grandfather's Clock' is located, is a 16th-century coaching inn on the banks of the Tees. It has comfortable lounges and bars, with roaring fires in the winter and a great garden for the warmer weather. You can eat in the bar or dine in the riverside restaurant, where well-cooked local food is available.

Magnesia Bank

Camden Street,
North Shields
NE30 1NH
Tel: 0191 257 4831;
www.magnesiabank.com
The Magnesia Bank is an award-winning real-ale pub with great food. Its beers come from a number of local microbreweries, including Wallsend Mordue Brewery. The food includes fresh local fish and steaks, plus home-made puddings. There are regular live music nights.

Victoria Inn

86 Hallgarth Street,
Durham DH1 3AS
Tel: 0191 386 5269;
www.victoriainn-durhamcity.
co.uk
The Victoria Inn opened in 1899. Its first customers would still recognize it, for the interior has changed very little. In this Victorian gem, complete with tiny partitioned spaces, there are real ales – a changing selection – and more than 70 types of whisky (and whiskey). The Victoria does not serve food.

Wear & Tees

The High Pennines – 'England's Last Wilderness' – combine the majestic sweep of high moorland with deep valleys where waterfalls thunder over sheer crags. The villages are peaceful now, but these were once thriving industrial centres. The area was the focus of Britain's lead-mining industry, and the deserted buildings and tall chimneys still punctuate the landscape as a reminder of those prosperous days. The dramatic scenery of Weardale and Teesdale characterises this remote and captivating region, where there are wide views and secret corners, small farms and few people.

10 Walk start point

ALLENHEADS

ALLENDALE

HARTHOPE MOOR

Unmissable attractions

Drive the road over Harthope Moor from St John's Chapel to Langdon Beck...walk the Pennine Way from Widdy Bank Farm to Cauldron Snout waterfall...see the mechanical swan swallow its silver fish in the Bowes Museum in Barnard Castle ...take a stroll round Blanchland and a snack at the Lord Crewe Arms...search for the elusive Teesdale violet in Upper Teesdale...enjoy the gardens and sumptuous interiors of Raby Castle...go fishing at Cow Green Reservoir...enjoy the solitude of the moorland landscape in Upper Weardale.

1 Harthope Moor
If you drive across Harthope Moor you will be navigating England's highest classified road. However, you might just decide to stop the car and enjoy the clear air as you explore on foot.

2 Pennine Way
Known as a challenging trek if you tackle the whole length of the Way, there are gentle and less demanding sections along the route.

3 Bowes Museum
This French-style building houses one of the country's best private art collections. The collector was one John Bowes, the illegitimate son of the 10th Duke of Strathmore. John and Josephine, his French wife, combined good taste and wealth to build up their unique collection.

4 Raby Castle Gardens
The beautiful castle of Raby is surrounded by equally attractive parkland. Deer roam in the park, and there are several different gardens to explore.

5 Cow Green Reservoir
This reservoir was built between 1967 and 1971 to supply Teesside's industry, in the face of opposition by environmentalists. Now well established, the lake is popular for fishing and the surrounding hills offer fine walking country.

ALLENDALE MAP REF NY8355

Set 800 feet (244m) up amongst the spectacular Pennine scenery, Allendale town (rather than the dale that bears its name) is the geographical centre of Britain – a sundial on the church gives its latitude. Its pretty market place is peaceful for most of the year but on New Year's Eve it becomes tumultuous at the annual Baal Fire celebration. With its origins back in the Dark Ages, perhaps celebrating the winter solstice, the event attracts hundreds of visitors. Brave men, called 'guysers', dress up in costume, blacken their faces, then carry blazing tar barrels around the town on their heads. At midnight a huge bonfire is lit.

Langley Castle, 3 miles (4.8km) north, was built in the 14th century, ruined by Henry IV in 1405 and well restored in 1890. It is now a hotel, but the grounds and the public rooms can be visited. The dale has not one, but two rivers – the East and West Allen – fed by many peaty burns that cascade down from the surrounding high hills.

■ Activity

WALKS IN THE WOODS

With much of Northumbria clothed in coniferous plantation, walking in mature, broad-leaved woodland is a particular pleasure. At Allen Banks, 5 miles (8km) north of Allendale town, the River Allen runs through a heavily wooded gorge, with beech and oak trees clinging to the hillsides. This is one of the rare places in Britain where you might see a red squirrel, though roe deer are normally much easier to spot. There is a suspension bridge to link the two sides of the gorge, and in Morralee Wood is a tarn.

ALLENHEADS MAP REF NY8645

The East Allen Mine was once the most important source of lead in Europe, and local landowners developed Allenheads as a model village, with a school, a library, a church and a chapel. Lead mining ended in the late 19th century, and now the village welcomes tourists – Allenheads Heritage Centre provides an excellent introduction to the area.

At the realistically named Killhope Lead Mining Centre, 2.5 miles (4km) southwest of Allenheads across the County Durham boundary, the restored 1870s lead-crushing mill, with its huge overshot waterwheel, brings Victorian mining to life. You can also learn about lead mining at the Nenthead Mines Heritage Centre near Alston, where you can also pan for gold!

BARNARD CASTLE

MAP REF NZ0516

Visitors to 'Barney' often ask 'Where's the castle?', for it is hidden from most of the town. It occupies a site high above the Tees on the west side. Bernard (Barnard) Baliol first fortified the site, and parts of his 12th-century castle still exist, rebuilt when the Bishops of Durham and the Nevilles held it. Anne Neville married Richard III in 1472 and so brought the castle into his ownership.

The main surviving parts can be seen around the Inner Ward, among them the 14th-century Round Tower and also the 15th-century Great Chamber – notice the boar badge of King Richard. The Tees, crossed by the County Bridge of 1569 below the castle, used to be the boundary between Yorkshire and County

Visit

RABY CASTLE

Raby Castle, northeast of Barnard Castle, may be on the site of King Canute's palace. It is one of the most beautifully positioned castles in the country, with nine towers and battlements overlooking the lake, and superb gardens to offset its warlike appearance. When the castle was restored by John Carr in the 1760s, a long tunnel was created so that carriages could drive through the Lower Hall and out under the Chapel Tower. Carr re-created the interiors, too – his entrance hall is impressive – and from the 1840s come the stunning French-style Octagon Room and the Baron's Hall. The gardens have a number of rare trees and shrubs, including a fig tree planted in 1768.

Insight

BOWES VENTURE

John Bowes was the son of the 10th Earl of Strathmore – who neglected to marry John's mother. John inherited huge estates in County Durham from his mother, and became a respected MP, industrialist and collector. He married a French actress, Josephine Coffin-Chevallier. She had superb taste, he had money and organisational skills, and together they amassed the collection that became the Bowes Museum. Sadly, neither lived to see the museum open.

Insight

A ROMANTIC HEROINE

The ghost of Dorothy Forster is said to haunt the Lord Crewe Arms in Blanchland, and to roam the moors above. The niece of Lord Crewe, Bishop of Durham, she was a real-life heroine who rode, in disguise, from here to London to rescue her brother, who was imprisoned in the Tower for his part in the Jacobite uprising under Lord Derwentwater.

Durham. In the former bridge chapel, lying outside the jurisdiction of both the Bishop of Durham and the Archbishop of York, illegal weddings took place.

The town's wide streets – Galgate and Horse Market – were full of animals for sale in the past, and the busy Market Place falls gently to the Market Cross, a handsome octagon built in 1747. The colonnade provided shelter to the butter sellers, and the upper floor was the town hall. Notice the bullet holes in the weather vane, made in an 1804 shooting contest. Beyond the Market Cross, The Bank was once the foremost shopping street. Its oldest building, Blagroves House, boasts a tall bay window and the jolly figure of a musician over the door. Thorngate and Bridgegate comprised the industrial area of the town in the 18th and 19th centuries – the mill buildings and weavers' cottages, with their long upper windows, survive.

East of The Bank is The Demesnes, an area of open land which used to supply the town with water from many springs. Newgate, with the parish church, leads to Barnard Castle's greatest surprise, the Bowes Museum. Housed in a French-style château, it is one of the most remarkable private art collections in all of Europe, with Roman altars, porcelain, paintings by both Goya and El Greco, costumes, toys, musical instruments, furniture, complete rooms from demolished buildings...don't miss the mechanical swan, which twice a day will preen itself and eat the silver fish swimming in its stream.

Egglestone Abbey, 1.25 miles (2km) southeast of Barnard Castle, was founded by Premonstratensian Canons in about 1196 – they were known as the White Canons, and they lived a strict and severe life in the abbey. The ruins are very beautiful, with parts of the church still standing, although the Canons' living quarters have survived less well. In 1548 the abbey, minus its Canons, was sold to Robert Strelley, who made part of the cloisters into an Elizabethan house – now itself a ruin.

BLANCHLAND MAP REF NY9650

It is easier to believe that Blanchland was once home to the sombre white-robed Premonstratensian Canons who founded the abbey in 1165 and gave the village its name, than to generations of workers from the nearby lead mines. This is because Blanchland is regarded as one of the most perfect villages in England – a cluster of stone houses, which glow golden in the sunlight, set in a deep, lush, wooded valley among high moorland. Most of the cottages were built in the mid-18th century for Lord Crewe, Bishop of Durham, who owned the estate. When the mines had closed and the miners departed, Blanchland remained in the hands of the Crewe Trustees, undisturbed in its beauty.

In the centre of the village is the L-shaped square, which may have been the monastic courtyard. It is reached from the north through the 15th-century gatehouse, complete with battlements, and from the south over the bridge – the best views of the village are from here.

Part of the church ruins were well restored in the 18th century – you enter under the tower into the north transept,

■ Insight

A MORAL VEIN

In the mid-19th century, 90 per cent of all workers in Middleton-in-Teesdale were employed in the lead-mining industry – most of them working for The London Lead Mining Company. It opened its North of England headquarters here in 1815 and developed the town rapidly. The Quaker company had a paternalistic attitude, providing homes for its workers, education for their children, a library in Middleton House and encouragement for town activities like the band. It also encouraged the chapels, and insisted that every boy who wanted a job had to have a proper course of religious instruction. Foreign imports ended this beneficial despotism, and the company went bankrupt in 1905.

and turn under the crossing for the rest of the building, tall and light. Notice, on the floor, the grave slabs of the abbots, carved with their mitres, and of foresters with horns. The picturesque Lord Crewe Arms next door was the Abbot's Lodge. Portraits of Lord Crewe, his wife Dorothy Forster and his niece, the other Dorothy, can be found here. The garden was the cloister of the Abbey.

MIDDLETON-IN-TEESDALE
MAP REF NY9425

Middleton is the centre for exploring the wild landscapes of Upper Teesdale. Its stone-built houses are largely from the town's heyday as the centre of the dale's lead-mining industry. It is still possible to imagine it full of 19th-century miners. Its earlier history can be appreciated from the little bell-tower of 1567, like a garden summerhouse, in the corner of the

churchyard, away from the Victorian church. The London Lead Mining Company's Middleton House, with its fine clock-towered stable, is up the hill to the northwest, and the company's housing estate, Masterman Place, to the east of the town, is approached through a grand archway. In 1877 the Company Superintendent, Mr Bainbridge, gave a jolly cast-iron fountain to the town; it can be seen in Horsemarket.

Upstream from Middleton the River Tees becomes increasingly spectacular. The Visitor Centre at Bowlees, 3 miles (4.8km) northwest, provides an excellent introduction to the geology, archaeology, flora and wildlife of Upper Teesdale. There is a picnic site near by, and you can walk to Gibson's Cave, where 20-foot (6m) Summerhill Force has formed a hollow in the soft rock beneath.

Over the Tees is Wynch Bridge, Europe's earliest suspension bridge, originally built for miners in the 1740s, then rebuilt in 1828. It is 70 feet (21.4m) long, and only 2 feet (61cm) wide. Just above the bridge is Low Force, a series of picturesque waterfalls. Best of all is High Force, 1.5 miles (2.4km) further on and reached by a path through woods opposite the hotel – there is a good car park and a picnic area. The Tees plunges over the Great Whin Sill here, and roars into the huge gorge, at 70 feet (21.4m) the highest single-drop waterfall in England. Cauldron Snout, reached from Langdon Beck, is England's longest cascade. There are spectacular basalt cliffs in the narrow valley below, and rare Arctic plants on the sugar limestone of Widdybank Fell.

ST JOHN'S CHAPEL
MAP REF NY8837

St John's Chapel in Weardale can be reached by the highest classified road in England, over Harthope Moor from Teesdale. The church, overlooking the small square with its diminutive Town Hall, was rebuilt in 1752 with impressive classical columns to be seen inside. There are pleasant footpaths all around, and access across a footbridge to the Weardale Way. At Ireshopeburn, a mile (1.6km) west, is the Weardale Museum, in a former manse, with reconstructions of Dale life around 1870. Next door is the 18th-century chapel where John Wesley preached and a room in the museum is dedicated to him and his work.

The market town of Stanhope, lower down the valley amid woodland, is known as the Capital of Weardale. By the churchyard entrance is a fossilised tree-stump, said to be 250 million years old. Rather less ancient were the entire possessions of a Bronze Age family that were found in Heathery Burn Cave in 1850. Now in the British Museum, they showed early use of wheeled vehicles and horses. Another transportation method, the Heritage Line railway, runs regular trains on the branch line from Stanhope to Bishop Auckland.

Stanhope has an open-air swimming pool, and there are stepping stones set across the Tees to riverside walks. The Durham Dales Centre combines craft shops and a tea room with the Tourist Information Centre. On the first weekend in September at Wolsingham, 6 miles (9.6km) west, the oldest agricultural show in England is held annually.

Barnard Castle

Approach Barnard Castle from Bowes and you'll see the imposing nature of its fortress, which tops a bold 80 foot (25m) crag and towers above the River Tees. In 1292 the little town that had grown around the castle was granted a charter for a market. The medieval layout of streets, yards and back alleys still exists today. On the walk by the Tees you'll see grey marble riverbeds, a stone that has supplied building material for the locals. Abbey Bridge takes you across the river, which has formed a deep gorge, and gives you a closer look at the old abbey. A quiet lane takes you past Bow Bridge. Just beyond this you're back on field paths above the Tees.

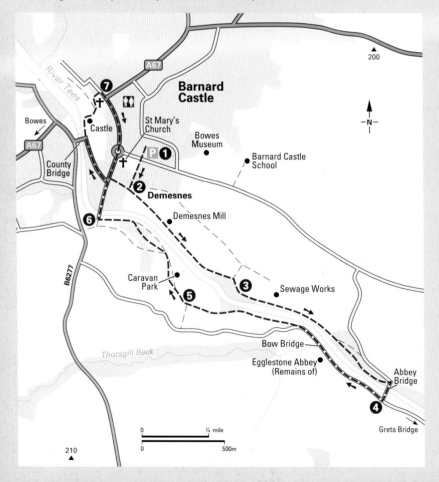

Route Directions

1 From the car park go through the passageway signposted for the river. Go across Newgate Street and continue through another little ginnel, which leads through the churchyard of St Mary's, then out on to the riverside parkland of Demesnes.

2 Here turn left along a stony path, which angles down to the river. It passes Demesnes Mill, then follows the north bank of the Tees, with the river on your right.

3 You pass (quickly if the wind is in the wrong direction) the sewage works. Ignore the upper left fork of two paths and stay by the river to enter pretty woodland, which allows glimpses of the remains of Egglestone Abbey on the far banks. Go through the gate on to the road and turn right over Abbey Bridge.

4 Turn right at the junction on the far side of the bridge, then go left up the access track to view the abbey. Return to the road and follow it left, to pass Bow Bridge. A squeeze stile in the hedge on the right marks the start of the path along the south bank of the Tees. On the approach to a caravan park the path crosses fields and veers slightly away from the river.

5 Turn right along a surfaced track, down to the caravan park and take the second drive on the left, which eventually leads to a continuation of the riverside path.

6 Turn right over the footbridge back into Barnard Castle and go straight ahead into Thorngate. Turn left along Bridgegate. Where the road crosses the County Bridge, go straight on to follow a path that rounds the castle walls to the entrance. After visiting the castle, continue past the Methodist church to the start of Galgate.

7 Turn right along Horse Market and continue to the Market Cross. Carry on down The Bank then, at the top of Thorngate, go left to Demesnes. Retrace your earlier steps back to the car park at the start of the walk.

Route facts

DISTANCE/TIME
4.25 miles (6.8km) 2h30

MAP OS Explorer OL31 North Pennines

START Car park (pay-and-display) at end of Queen Street, grid ref: NZ 051163

TRACKS Town streets and good paths, 6 stiles

GETTING TO THE START
Barnard Castle lies on the A67, 15 miles (24km) west of Darlington. From the centre of town, turn off the A67 onto King Street and then turn right onto Queen Street. The car park is at the end of the road.

THE PUB The Morritt Arms, Greta Bridge (3 miles/ 4.8km southeast).
Tel: 01833 627232

What to look for

The historic County Bridge, located beneath the castle, has different kinds of stonework on its upper and lower parts. This unusual feature is the result of water damage caused by the great floods of 1661. The flood waters left the south bank of the river so eroded that travellers were required to climb a ladder in order to get themselves on to the bridge. Before these floods, the bridge was known for having a built-in chapel where the nefarious Bible clerk Cuthbert Hilton carried out numerous illegal marriage ceremonies.

■ TOURIST INFORMATION CENTRES

Barnard Castle
Woodleigh, Flatts Road.
Tel: 01833 690909

Middleton-in-Teesdale
10 Market Place.
Tel: 01833 641001

Stanhope
Durham Dales Centre.
Tel: 01388 527650

■ PLACES OF INTEREST

Allenheads Heritage Centre
Tel: 01434 685586

Bowes Castle
Tel: 0191 269 1200;
www.english-heritage.org.uk
Free.

The Bowes Museum
Barnard Castle.
Tel: 01833 690606; www.
thebowesmuseum.org.uk

Bowlees Picnic Area and Visitor Centre
Middleton-in-Teesdale.
Tel: 01833 622292;
www.durhamwt.myzen.org.uk
Free.

Barnard Castle
Tel: 01833 638212;
www.english-heritage.org.uk

Durham Dales Centre
Castle Gardens, Stanhope.
Tel: 01388 527650; www.
durhamdalescentre.co.uk
Free.

Egglestone Abbey
Barnard Castle. Free.
Tel: 0191 269 1200;
www.english-heritage.org.uk

Eggleston Hall Gardens
Eggleston, Barnard Castle.
Tel: 01833 650115;
www.egglestonhall.co.uk

Gaunless Valley Visitor Centre
Butterknowle.
Tel: 01833 690909
Free.

High Force
Near Middleton-in-Teesdale.
England's highest waterfall.
Tel: 01833 622209;
www.rabycastle.com

Killhope Lead Mining Centre
Tel: 01388 537505;
www.killhope.org.uk

Raby Castle
Tel: 01833 660202;
www.rabycastle.com
Magnificent 14th-century
castle with a deer park, lakes
and walled garden.

Rokeby Park
Rokeby, Barnard Castle.
Tel: 01609 748612;
www.rokebypark.com

Thorpe Farm Centre
Thorpe Farm, Greta Bridge.
Tel: 01833 627242;
www.thorpefarm.co.uk
Falconry and children's play
area (free), bistro and shops.

Tow Law Beehive Coke Ovens
Inkerman. Free.
Tel: 0191 269 1239

Weardale Railway
Wolsingham to Stanhope.
Tel: 0845 600 1348;
www.weardale-railway.org.uk

■ FOR CHILDREN

Durham Dales Centre
Castle Gardens, Stanhope.
Tel: 01388 527650;
www.durhamdalescentre.
co.uk. Free.

■ SHOPPING

Barnard Castle
Market, Wed. Farmers'
market, 1st Sat of month.

LOCAL SPECIALITIES

Arts and Crafts
Middleton Crafts
1c Chapel Row,
Middleton-in-Teesdale.
Tel: 07776 144897

Landscape & Wildlife Painting
Andy Beck, Newgate Gallery,
6 The Bank, Barnard Castle.
Tel: 01833 695201;
www.theteesdalegallery.co.uk

Cheese
Cotherstone cheese is
available from several outlets
in and near Barnard Castle.

■ SPORTS & ACTIVITIES

ABSEILING, CAVING & CLIMBING
Kingsway Adventure Centre,
Alston Road, Middleton-in-
Teesdale. Tel: 01833 640881;
www.kingswaycentre.co.uk

ANGLING
Contact local Tourist
Information Centres and
fishing tackle shops. Some
local Post Offices sell
permits.

ARCHERY

Kingsway Adventure Centre,
Alston Road,
Middleton-in-Teesdale.
Tel: 01833 640881;
www.kingswaycentre.co.uk

CANOEING

Permits required; contact
local Tourist Information
Centres.
Teesdale Canoe Club,
Barnard Castle.
Tel: 01833 650691
Kingsway Adventure Centre,
Alston Road,
Middleton-in-Teesdale.
Tel: 01833 640881;
www.kingswaycentre.co.uk

COUNTRY PARKS & FORESTS

Pow Hill Country Park, near
Derwent Reservoir.
Hamsterley Forest – many
paths and trails and Visitor
Centre.

CYCLE HIRE

Hamsterley

Wood n' Wheels,
Hamsterley Forest, Redford.
Tel: 01388 488222;
www.woodnwheels.co.uk

Wolsingham

Dale Bike Hire,
8 Ward Terrace.
Tel: 01388 527737;
www.dalebikehire.co.uk

HORSE-RIDING

Lartington

Raygill Riding Centre,
Raygill Farm.
Tel: 01833 688739;
www.raygillriding.co.uk

Allendale

Sinderhope Trekking Centre,
High Sinderhope.
Tel: 01434 685266;
www.sinderhopepony
trekking.co.uk

SAILING

Derwent Reservoir
Sailing Club.
Tel: 01434 675033;
www.drsc.co.uk
Teesdale Sailing Club,
Grassholme Reservoir.
Tel: 01888 451215;
www.teesdalesc.org.uk

SKIING

Nov–Easter, snow permitting.
Contact Barnard Castle
Tourist Information Centre.

WATERSKIING

Balderhead Reservoir.
Tel: 01748 824271 (evenings)
or 01833 650310 (weekends).

WINDSURFING

Teesdale Sailing Club,
Selset Reservoir.
Tel: 01748 823953/823114;
www.teesdalesc.or.uk

LONG-DISTANCE FOOTPATHS

Lead-mining trail. A 24-mile
(38km) walk from Cowshill to
Edmundbyers.
Teesdale Way. A 92-mile
(148km) walk from Dufton to
Warrenby, Redcar, linking
with the Pennine Way.
Weardale Way. A 77-mile
(124km) walk from Wearhead
to Monkwearmouth.

**■ ANNUAL EVENTS
& CUSTOMS**

Allendale

Allendale Fair, late May.
Agricultural Show, mid-Aug.
Baal Fire Celebration,
New Year's Eve.

Barnard Castle

Meet Weekend, late May.
Steam Fair, late May.
Truck Show, late Aug.

Bowes

Agricultural Show, early Sep.

Eastgate

Spring Sheep Show,
late May.

Eggleston

Eggleston Agricultural Show,
mid-Sep.

St John's Chapel

Weardale Agricultural Show,
late Aug.

Stanhope

Agricultural Show, early Sep.

BLANCHLAND

Tea Rooms

Allendale Tearooms

Market Place, Allendale
Town NE47 9BD
Tel: 01434 683575; www.
allendaletearooms.co.uk
In the centre of town, the
beamed tea rooms were built
in the 1840s and retain their
early-Victorian atmosphere.
The counter has a vast
display of home-made cakes
and scones, and you can also
feast on steak pies, pasties
and an ever-changing choice
of specials from the board.
The tea rooms also serve a
good, wholesome Sunday
lunch – best to book.

The Market
Place Teashop

29 Market Place,
Barnard Castle DL12 8NE
Tel: 01833 690110;
www.teashop-barnard-
castle.co.uk
The Market Place Teashop
is in a superb 17th-century
building, complete with
flagged floors and bare walls.
There is a wide selection of
cakes and scones, all
properly served by polite,
uniformed waitresses; you
can also have a more
substantial lunch here.
Among the specialities are
Yorkshire curd tarts and
pies, including bilberry.
Closed on Sunday.

The White Monk
Tearooms

The Old School,
Blanchland DH8 9ST
Tel: 01434 675044
Located in the heart of the
lovely village of Blanchland,
the White Monk Tearooms
occupy the former village
school. There are two loft
rooms and a garden.
Home-made scones with
cream and jam, as well as
delicious cakes (try the coffee
and walnut) are on the menu.
Simple lunches are served.

Pubs

Black Bull Inn

Bridge End, Frosterley
DL13 2SL
Tel: 01388 527784
This isn't the poshest pub,
but it is worth seeking out. As
well as good local ales, it
serves real cider and great
food. Using local ingredients,
the chef conjures up dishes
like white fish, prawn, crab,
date and fennel stew and
roasts, Wensleydale cheese
and apple flan and orange
and ginger cake. Open
Thursday to Sunday.

The Lord Crewe Arms

Blanchland, DH8 9SP
Tel: 01434 675251;
www.lordcrewehotel.com
The Lord Crewe Arms was
once the abbot's house for
the adjoining abbey. Now it's
a comfortable hotel with
flagged floors, antiques and
log fires, where relaxation
comes easily. You can eat in
the bar, or out in the garden
in summer, or more formally
in the restaurant. The food is
excellent – traditional British
and locally sourced.

Morritt Arms Hotel

Great Bridge, Barnard Castle
DL12 9SE. Tel: 01833 627232;
www.themorritt.co.uk
Charles Dickens stayed here
as he researched *Nicholas
Nickleby* in 1839. Now the
hotel's interior is comfortably
modern. The Dickens Bar has
real ales and bar snacks. The
formal restaurant and the
bistro offer great choices
Steaks are to the fore on the
menu, but there are good
choice for fish-eaters and
vegetarians. For pudding, try
the pear in honey and saffron.

The Wallace Arms

Rowfoot, Featherstone
NE49 0JF
Tel: 01434 321872
This traditional place serves
good, simple food. There is
plenty of fresh fish, like
haddock in beer batter, as
well as steaks and pies.
Snacks and sandwiches,
vegetarian dishes and a
children's menu are available.

■ TOURIST INFORMATION CENTRES

Stella House, Goldcrest Way, Newburn Riverside, Newcastle upon Tyne. Tel: 0191 229 6200; www.newcastlegateshead.com www.visitnorthumberland.com www.thisisdurham.com www.visitnortheastengland.com

Durham Wildlife Trust
Rainton Meadows, Chilton Moor, Houghton-le-Spring. Tel: 0191 584 3112; www.durhamwt.myzen.co.uk

English Heritage
Tel: 0870 333 1181; www.english-heritage.org.uk

Forest Enterprise
Kielder Forest District, Eals Burn, Bellingham. Tel. 01434 220242 www.forestry.gov.uk

National Trust
Scots' Gap, Morpeth. Tel: 01670 774691; www.nationaltrust.org.uk

Northumberland National Park
Eastburn, South Park, Hexham Tel: 01434 605555; www. northumberlandnationalpark. org.uk

Northumberland Wildlife Trust
Garden House, St Nicholas Park, Jubilee Road, Newcastle upon Tyne. Tel: 0191 284 6884; www.nwt.org.uk

Northumbria Water
Abbey Road, Pity Me, Durham. Tel: 0870 608 4820; www.nwl.co.uk

■ OTHER INFORMATION

BEACHES

Alnmouth
Wide stretch of sand at low tide. Bathing not advised.

Bamburgh and Seahouses
Fine stretches of sandy beach with rocky outcrops. No dogs on small beach at Seahouses. Only safe to bathe on incoming tides due to strong currents.

Beadnell Bay
Sands curve 2 miles (3.2km) south. Dogs restricted on part of beach due to nesting birds.

Druridge Bay
Sands, dunes and grassland.

Embleton Bay
Wide, dune-fringed beach. Safe only when tide is coming in.

South Shields
Fine sandy beaches divided by rocky outcrops. Dogs restricted.

Spittal
Popular sandy beach at the mouth of the Tweed.

Sunderland
Extensive sands. Dogs restricted at Whitburn and Seaburn.

Warkworth
3 miles (4.8km) of wide, firm sands, backed by dunes to the north. No bathing at high tide.

Whitley Bay
Sandy beach. Dogs restricted.

PUBLIC TRANSPORT

Summer buses from Carlisle and Hexham serve the major sites along Hadrian's Wall, linking with services from Newcastle, Carlisle and Alston.

■ ORDNANCE SURVEY MAPS

THE COAST
Landranger 1:50,000;
Sheets 74, 75, 81
Explorer 325, 332, 339, 340, 346
Outdoor Leisure 16 1:25,000

THE HILLS
Landranger 1:50,000;
Sheets 74, 75, 80, 81, 87, 88
Explorer 339
Outdoor Leisure 16, 42, 43
1:25,000

ALONG HADRIAN'S WALL
Landranger 1:50,000;
Sheets 86, 87
Explorer 316
Outdoor Leisure 43 1:25,000

CITIES & SAINTS
Landranger 1:50,000;
Sheets 81, 87, 88, 92, 93
Explorer 304, 305, 306, 307, 308, 316, 325

WEAR & TEES
Landranger 1:50,000;
Sheets 86, 87, 88, 91, 92
Explorer 307
Outdoor Leisure 1:25,000
Sheets 19, 30, 31, 43

■ USEFUL WEBSITES

www.visitnortheastengland.com
www.visitsouthtyneside.co.uk
www.welcomenorthumberland.
com
www.northtyneside.gov.uk/
tourism
www.teesdalediscovery.com

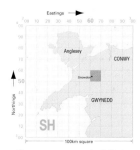

The National Grid system covers Great Britain with an imaginary network of grid squares. Each is 100km square in area and is given a unique alphabetic reference, as shown in the diagram above.

These squares are sub-divided into one hundred 10km squares, identified by vertical lines (eastings) and horizontal lines (northings). The reference for the square a feature is located within is made by adding the numbers of the two lines which cross in the bottom left corner of that square to the alphabetic reference (ignoring the small figures). The easting is quoted first. For example, SH6050.

For a 2-figure reference, the zeros are omitted, giving just SH65. In this book, we use 4-figure references, which allow us to pinpoint the feature more accurately by dividing the 10km square into one hundred 1km squares. These squares are not actually printed on the road atlas but are estimated by eye. The same process is carried out as before, giving an enhanced reference of SH6154.

Key to Atlas

▬M4▬	Motorway with number	
▬S▬ Fleet	Motorway service area	
▬▬▬	Motorway toll	
⬡	Motorway junction with and without number	
⬡	Restricted motorway junctions	
⬡	Motorway and junction under construction	
▬A3▬	Primary route single/dual carriageway	
BATH	Primary route destinations	
✛✛✛	Roundabout	
Y 5 Y	Distance in miles between symbols	
A1123	Other A Road single/dual carriageway	
B2070	B road single/dual carriageway	
▬▬▬	Unclassified road single/dual carriageway	
⊨═════	Road tunnel	

══Toll══	Toll
▄▄▄▄▄▄	Road under construction
▭▭▭▭▭	Narrow Primary route with passing places
➤	Steep gradient
○—×—	Railway station and level crossing
┼┼┼┼┼┼	Tourist railway
─ ─ ─ ─	National trail
⋯⋯⋯⋯	Forest drive
⌣⌣⌣	Heritage coast
⚓⚓	Ferry route
6	Walk start point
1	Cycle start point
3	Tour start point

⛪	Abbey, cathedral or priory
🐟	Aquarium
♜	Castle
◠	Cave
♕	Country park
⛊	County cricket ground
🐄	Farm or animal centre
✿	Garden
⚑	Golf course
⌂	Historic house
🐎	Horse racing
▣	Motor racing
🏛	Museum
⊕	Airport
Ⓗ	Heliport
✖	Windmill
NT	National Trust property

NTS	National Trust for Scotland property
🦅	Nature reserve
★	Other place of interest
P+R	Park and Ride location
♣	Picnic site
⚙	Steam centre
⛷	Ski slope natural
⛷	Ski slope artificial
ℤ	Tourist Information Centre
☼	Viewpoint
ℤ	Visitor or heritage centre
⚘	Zoological or wildlife collection
	Forest Park
	National Park (England & Wales)
	National Scenic Area (Scotland)

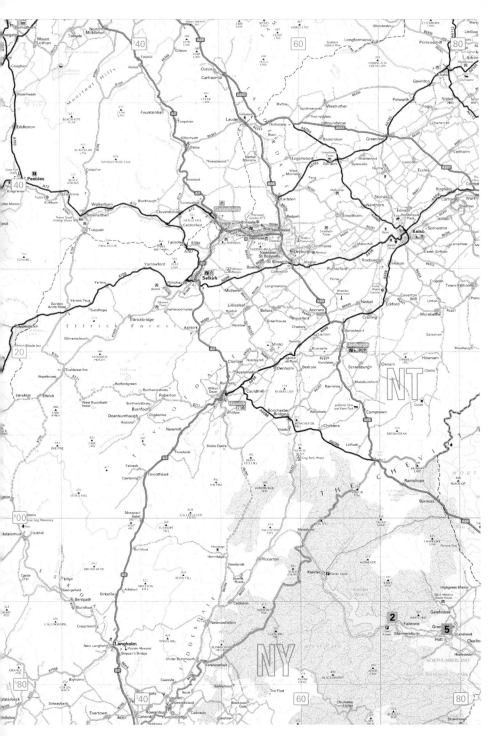

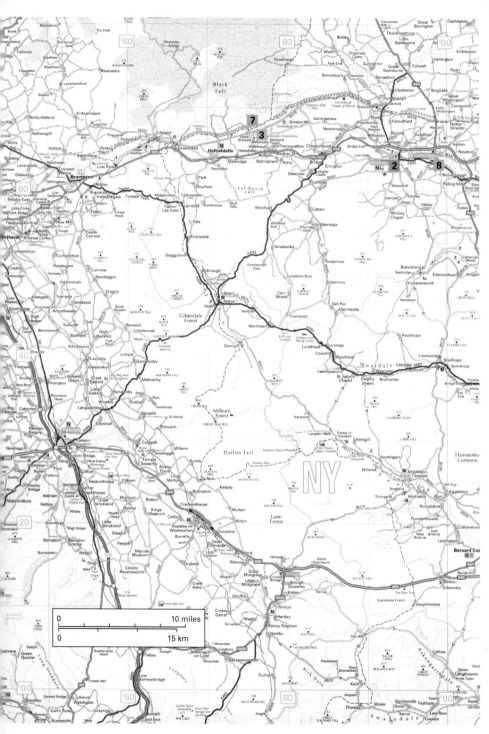

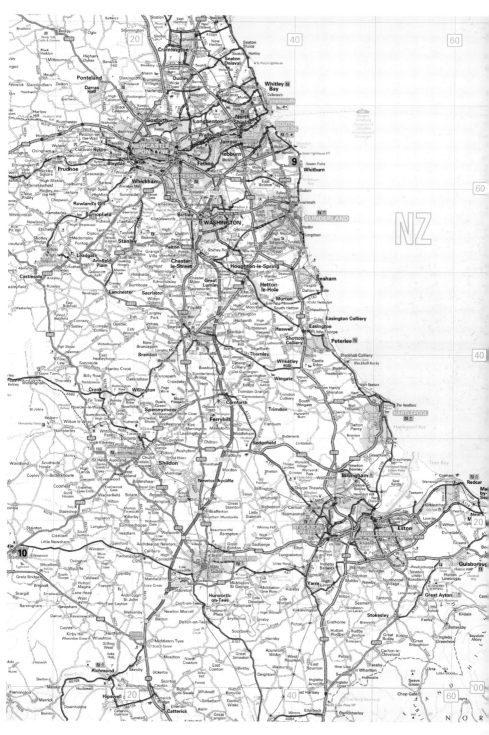

The Automobile Association would like to thank the following photographers and companies for their assistance in the preparation of this book. Abbreviations for the picture credits are as follows – (t) top; (b) bottom; (c) centre; (l) left; (r) right; (AA) AA World Travel Library

1 AA/Roger Coulam; 4/5 AA/Roger Coulam; 8t AA/Roger Coulam; 8bl AA/Roger Coulam; 8cr AA/Roger Coulam; 8br AA/Roger Coulam; 9c AA/Roger Coulam; 9b AA; 10t AA/Roger Coulam; 10c AA/Jeff Beazley; 10b AA/Roger Coulam; 11t AA/Roger Coulam; 11b AA/Roger Coulam; 13 AA/Jeff Beazley; 14t AA/Roger Coulam; 14b AA/Jeff Beazley; 18/19 AA/Cameron Lees; 21t AA/Jeff Beazley; 21b AA/Roger Coulam; 22cl AA/Jeff Beazley; 22bl AA/Roger Coulam; 22r © Mike Kipling Photography/Alamy; 23t AA/Roger Coulam; 23c AA/Roger Coulam; 23b AA/Jeff Beazley; 26 AA/Jeff Beazley; 31 AA/Roger Coulam; 38 © Troy GB images/Alamy; 46 AA/Roger Coulam; 48/49 AA/Roger Coulam; 51t AA/Roger Coulam; 51bl AA/Jeff Beazley; 51br AA/Roger Coulam; 52c AA/S & O Mathews; 52b AA/Roger Coulam; 53t AA/Roger Coulam; 53c AA/Cameron Lees; 53b AA/Roger Coulam; 55 © Mark Sunderland/Alamy; 60/61 AA/Roger Coulam; 64 AA/Roger Coulam; 69 AA/Roger Coulam; 70 AA/Roger Coulam; 78 AA/Roger Coulam; 80/81 AA/Roger Coulam; 82 AA/N Setchfield 83t AA/Roger Coulam; 83b © Jason Friend/Alamy; 84c AA/Roger Coulam; 84b © Trinity Mirror/Mirrorpix/Alamy; 85t AA/Cameron Lees; 85c AA/Roger Coulam; 85b AA/Roger Coulam; 87 AA/Roger Coulam; 96 AA/Roger Coulam; 102/3 AA/Roger Coulam; 108 AA/Jeff Beazley; 110/111 AA/Roger Coulam; 113 AA/Roger Coulam; 114l AA/Roger Coulam; 114r AA/Roger Coulam; 115t AA/Roger Coulam; 115b AA/Jeff Beazley; 118 © Jeff Greenberg/Alamy; 123 AA/Roger Coulam; 126 © Stuart Forster/Alamy; 132 AA/Jeff Beazley; 134/135 AA/Roger Coulam; 137tl AA/Roger Coulam; 137tr AA/Roger Coulam; 137b AA/Roger Coulam; 138l AA/Roger Coulam; 138cr AA/Roger Coulam; 138br AA/Cameron Lees; 139t AA/Roger Coulam; 139b AA/Roger Coulam; 141 © Mark Sunderland/Alamy; 144 © Duncan Davis/Alamy; 150 AA/Jeff Beazley.

Every effort has been made to trace the copyright holders, and we apologise in advance for any accidental errors. We would be happy to apply the corrections in the following edition of this publication.